D0442214

IN STORE MARKETING

A NEW DIMENSION IN THE SHARE WARS

BY MICHAEL WAHL

INTRODUCTION BY:
John McKinnon

Dean, Babcock Graduate School of Management
Wake Forest University

In-Store Marketing
by Michael Wahl

Copyright © 1992 by Michael Wahl

All rights reserved. No part of this book may be reproduced in any form or by any electronic or mechanical means, including information storage and retrieval systems, without permission in writing from the author, except by a reviewer who may quote brief passages in a review.

Published by Sawyer Publishing Worldwide
529 Fifth Avenue
8th Floor
New York, NY 10017

Printed in the United States of America

Library of Congress Catalog Card Number 92-80956

ISBN: 0-9632764-0-9

For information on how to order additional copies,
please call (212) 714-6517

DEDICATION

This book is dedicated to all those people who make in-store marketing happen, the people behind the scenes, the designers, the marketeers and all those who really get into the trenches in what is becoming known as the STORE WARS.

ACKNOWLEDGEMENTS

There are many people who assisted me in the writing of this book — too many of them, in fact, to list on this page, but special recognition should be given to the following: Gordon Wade of the Cincinnati Consulting Group; Walt Pilcher of Pilcher Associates; Jacqueline Silverstein, my assistant, who worked through this book from the very beginning from tapes spontaneously dictated in planes, trains and automobiles; Carie Hodes who did so much in making all of this possible; Ellen Schmitz, our vice president of marketing, who supplied so much of the material; Roberta Robins for doing such a fine job of proofreading; Chuck Karel for his many hours of typing; and finally, Rob Stuart who designed the layout and graphics of this book.

CONTENTS

INTRODUCTION

by John McKinnon

Dean, Babcock Graduate School of Management
Wake Forest University

In *In-Store Marketing*, Mike Wahl suggests that 500 cursing parrots were partly responsible for creating the conditions that now make it so easy to shop for such items as pantyhose, cosmetics, refrigerated cookies, baby foods, puddings and lunch meats. That's a radical idea, isn't it? It sure gets your attention!

With the revolution currently taking place in marketing techniques, learning to do a better job of catching the attention of the retail consumer is what this book is all about.

Manufacturers and retailers of consumer packaged goods products have exhaustively studied the more popular elements of the marketing mix such as advertising, promotion, selling techniques, new product development, packaging and distribution. A successful career in marketing has required some expertise in each of these areas.

In the meantime, however, there have been some major changes in the balance that used to exist among these elements. As an example, advertising has become less effective and important as the Big Three networks' share of the TV audience has eroded with the emergence of Cable TV. As a result, and also due to the timely availability of more and better business information via the computer, the balance of power between retailer and manufacturer has shifted markedly towards the retailer. Instead of simply acting as conduits for moving products from manufacturer to consumer, retailers are now insisting on a higher dollar return for the "real estate" they are providing to manufacturers and are asserting their own marketing and merchandising objectives more firmly than ever before.

Promotion has become a distinct drain on profitability, requiring huge investments for share gains that are too often only marginal at best. Product proliferation has intensified the fight for shelf space. Clever package design is now the norm instead of the exception so a particular product rarely stands out from the crowd any more. Rising labor and energy costs, coupled with the growing demand for "quick response" delivery and reductions in working capital for inventory, have elevated distribution from a couple of annoying line items in the budget called freight and warehousing to the status of a major strategic issue.

The one thing that hasn't changed, however, except maybe to grow in importance by default is that there is still only one place that is the final venue of the consumer's purchase decision process and that's the store.

In this book, Mike Wahl, the chairman of The Howard Marlboro Group (or HMG) of New York, gives his insights into the whole arena of consumer marketing and more specifically, into in-store marketing. He describes in-store marketing as the new dimension in the share war.

Few people reading this book know Mike Wahl, but virtually everyone in this country, and quite a few in Europe, have been influenced by the work of his company. HMG, now a division of Saatchi and Saatchi, has created self-service retail displays that every American sees each time he or she shops—the L'eggs pantyhose rack, the Noxell cosmetics wall and the Pillsbury refrigerated dough center, among others. More than just displays, these are examples of a sub-segment of in-store marketing called category management that HMG may well have invented.

In-Store Marketing is both Mike Wahl's perceptions from over twenty years' involvement in in-store merchandising and his insights into the future of consumer marketing. These insights include his prognostications on how the revolutionary advances in information technology will help define the store of the future.

Marketing professionals and those just interested in marketing techniques can both enjoy and learn from *In-Store Marketing*.

PART I

Beginnings

CHAPTER ONE

Early Lessons: Adolph Hitler and The Little Drummer Boy

I'm sure Adolph Hitler didn't intend to be a benign influence on my life, but in a crazy way he was. He brought me to America. My parents escaped from Germany before the Kristallnacht, which marked the beginning of the long downhill slide into the tragedy of the Holocaust.

The night my father brought home the U.S. Visas, he and my mother decided the family must leave Heidelberg. To avoid arousing suspicion, they packed a single suitcase with a few warm clothes, some family pictures and all the money in the house... $117. They made a few guarded phone calls to relatives and friends, then drove to the railroad station and caught the night train to Bremerhaven. They left behind people they loved, the home they loved, the small manufacturing business my father had built, their language, their culture, their homeland... everything.

When I remember their courage, the life and death choice they made and the difficulties they faced in a new land, my problems always seem petty. Whenever I've taken risks others thought unwise, the enormous ones taken by my parents have brought a sense of proportion. Compared to their decision to leave Germany with $117, whatever risks I have taken in business have seemed, well, insignificant.

If Hitler was perversely responsible for my coming to America, it was a child, whose name I'll never know, who was responsible for sparking within me the desire to sell things, a desire which even now fills me with excitement each time I walk through the doors of The Howard Marlboro Group.

When I was six, I used to accompany my father when he made his weekly Sunday morning trip from Queens into Manhattan's Lower East Side to buy the next week's supply of neckties and shirts. At that time, he was selling office to office near our home in a working-class section of Jamaica, Queens.

How does one describe the excitement of the Lower East Side pushcart bazaars during World War II? For me it was a circus, a mystery movie, a State Fair, a trip to a foreign country, all crammed into a wonderful Disney World called Delancey Street. My father's source of supply was Abraham, a giant, hoarse-voiced, Orthodox Jew dressed in black. I'd never seen a beard like his before, and I was frightened and curious all at the same time. But more interesting was the fact that a youngster about my own age (Abraham's son? his grandson? an orphan off the streets?) was stationed in front of the stall. Except for the beard, he was a miniature version of Abraham — same black gown and skullcap, same soft ringlets in front of his ears. What's more, he had a drum which he beat steadily with one hand while his other hand rhythmically shook a tambourine. Boom/zing, boom/zing, boom/zing — slow, steady, repetitive. I was fascinated and envious. More envious than I'd been of my friends in kindergarten who were driven to school in new cars and seemed to have different clothes for each day of the week. More envious than I'd been of the boy next door who could always pay for ice cream when the Good Humor man came around.

I envied this strange-looking drummer boy. He had a job, a purpose. He'd found an important place in the world of grown-ups.

I couldn't get his image or the sound of his drum out of my mind. On the subway ride home, I asked my father about him. "He's Abraham's nephew," my father said, "and he's there to draw attention to the stall. He heard somewhere that in America, salesmen are called drummers, so he figured a real 'drummer' would be a good way to drum up business for his uncle. It's a gimmick."

Maybe it was just a gimmick, but to me it had mystery and excitement. It made Abraham's stall special and better than all the others. I decided I liked Abraham more than I feared him. The next week I

2

went back again with my father. This time I asked if I, too, could have some ties to sell. Abraham didn't laugh, scowl or even look surprised. Instead, he made me a proposition. I could take a dozen ties of different colors. He wouldn't charge me the $10 a dozen then but would trust me until the following week. If I could sell them at $1.50 or $2 each, I'd have a nice profit. Any ties I couldn't sell I was to return to him in good condition the following week.

I accepted, tucked the ties safely under my arm in a Macy's box and went to lunch with my father at a Horn & Hardart near the subway. He wanted to know why I wanted the ties and how I would go about selling them. I told him I wanted to make money for ice cream, but looking back now, I think the real reason was I wanted to be like the drummer boy, to do something important, something that mattered.

The actual selling of the ties turned out to be the easy part. After school the next day, I got on the trolley which ran from Richmond Hill to Jamaica. At that time, Jamaica was the last large town on Long Island. It was full of stores and offices. I headed for the biggest office building which housed many lawyers and insurance agents. I picked a floor and started to sell the ties door to door. It all seemed pretty simple, but even then, I had the clear sense that I had a "gimmick" of my own — no drum, no tambourine, no funny skullcap. My gimmick was the fact that I was a six-year-old in short pants.

The secretaries and switchboard operators in the front of each office often laughed when I pushed through the door with the box of ties under my arm. Usually they'd agree to send me in to talk with the lawyers and insurance brokers. I talked about colors and materials with those businessmen, and soon I began to get the feeling they were treating me the way grown-ups treat kids in the movies but never in real life. I was making a big hit, and I loved it.

I quickly increased the price from $1.50 to $2.50, and sold my dozen ties that morning. When I counted my money, I had over $20 — a clear profit of $10 for just a couple of hours' work! Even today, $10 would be an outstanding sum of money for a six-year-old to bring home. But in those days, when five cents bought you a Hershey bar or a subway ride into Manhattan, $10 was a fortune.

I couldn't wait to go home and tell my father the news, but he seemed quite upset by the whole thing. He explained to me that what he was trying to do was build a better future for mother and me. He hadn't brought us all the way from Germany to America for me to become a door-to-door salesman. My mother sided with me, and at last my father agreed that if I continued to do well in school, he'd allow me to go on with my tie business.

So I continued to do this on and off for a number of years whenever I needed money. But the older I got, the more difficult it became to get past the secretaries. I was losing my "gimmick."

When the tie business really began to wear thin, I started looking around for other opportunities. I had an aunt who knitted baby booties in immense quantities. To this day, nobody knows why she only made baby booties, but I suspect it was the only thing she knew how to knit. I asked her if I could buy them from her and then sell them, and how much she wanted for each pair. She only charged me $.50 a pair — probably just about the cost of the wool. I took the booties and started trying to sell them to the same people who had been buying my neckties. I flopped badly. I couldn't understand why a man who had been happy to buy a necktie didn't also want to buy booties. The ties, after all, were no different from any he could find in a dozen stores, but the booties were unique and beautifully made.

One day, as I was walking down the street, the answer suddenly came to me. I saw a man carrying artistically arranged flowers, and on them was a big sign, "Congratulations." I spoke to the man and asked him, "Congratulations for what?"

"My wife just had a baby," he explained, "and I'm on my way to see her in the hospital."

Click!

I pulled out a pair of my booties. I didn't have to say a thing. He said they were wonderful, that his wife would love them, and he paid me $2 for them. I realized I had now discovered the perfect market for baby booties. I visited every florist I could find in Queens, and most of them agreed that a lot of their customers would like to send along booties with their flowers. I made deals with several florists to supply them with booties. My aunt knitted prodigiously day and night, and I sold hundreds of baby booties until she moved to New

4

Orleans and removed my cheap supply source.

Today, as I go about my work in the HMG headquarters, I sometimes recall the Little Drummer Boy and my early career as a tie and bootie salesman, and I realize that many of the lessons I later applied with great success to building HMG were learned from those experiences. To wit:

- Make noise. Even people who don't know you or like you will come to your stall to see what all the racket is about.

- Keep making noise. Some people will buy in the hope of shutting you up; others will be new people who didn't hear the noise the first time.

- Be visually different, like the small Hasidic drummer boy or the six-year-old tie salesman in short pants.

- Pay your suppliers on time, especially if they are your aunt or a large Orthodox Jew with a beard!

- Go directly to your market, because you learn most about what your customers want and what they don't want from firsthand observation.

- Get a new gimmick, and when one no longer works, change it.

- Seek out target markets — 99 people out of 100 won't buy booties, but a new father or grandparent will buy 100 times out of 100.

CHAPTER TWO
Building a Business

How Do You Build a Successful Business?

I've been asked this question a lot, and I've come to the conclusion that basically it takes four things:

- An overwhelming desire to be the best at what you do. This means long hours of effort, and you must love what you are doing. Very few people get rich running businesses they hate.

- Nerve, guts, chutzpah. Everyone who has built a successful business can point to a few specific instances when he or she took a ground-breaking risk (behold the turtle, he only makes progress when he sticks his neck out).

- Ethics. By this I mean more than abiding by legal contracts. I mean fairness to employees, loyalty to friends and sharing financial rewards with others.

- Creativity. No one gets rich doing things the same way as everyone else. Now I admit HMG is in a business where creativity plays a very large part in everything we do, but the fact is, every business will benefit from a little creativity.

Let me illustrate with some real life examples.

Decide To Be The Best: The Ballad of Jimmy Lee

A couple of years ago, a letter arrived carrying a Chicago postmark and a big, red "Urgent" stamp. Susie, my secretary, had attached a note saying I'd get a kick out of reading it.

"Dear Mr. Wahl,

"You met me back in July when you and a photographer from your company were trying to find out how we set up our frozen food cases at a supermarket in Chicago. I'm the Chinese-American stock boy you talked with, and you said I knew my business and was a big help to you.

"... I've been a stock boy every summer while going through Northwestern majoring in pre-law. The law is my family's idea. I want to get into retailing ... and you're the first man I ever actually met who seemed to be as excited as I am about what can be done. I was too embarrassed to ask you then, but now I will:

"... Are there any opportunities at your company (or do you know of anyplace else) where somebody like me could get started putting my ideas about how stores should be run to work? I've made notes about dozens of ways supermarkets could improve, and I just want a chance to talk about my ideas with you. If you like them, maybe you'd be willing to hire me or recommend me to some other company.

"... I'm going to visit New York next week, and I hope you'll be willing to spend just a few minutes with me to tell me whether my ideas are any good."

He signed it, "Your sincere admirer," and in the postscript said he was a good photographer and would bring along some pictures he took in the store.

That "sincere admirer" business tickled me. Usually my "BS" detector goes off when someone who wants something pays me a compliment. But this was so direct, so bold, it made me smile. Susie was right; I did get a kick out of this note. It reminded me of when I was in my teens and had a head and gut exploding with ideas on how the bastard of a butcher I was then working for could expand his business. I told Susie that if Jimmy Lee actually did call, I'd be happy to see him.

He called that same afternoon and was in our reception area just before five. I went out to personally take him on the "client tour."

Most high-powered advertising agencies decorate their walls with neatly framed examples of their multi-million dollar campaigns. These are intended to intimidate small accounts and to tell the big prospects, "Hey, if we're good enough for du Pont or U.S. Steel, we're certainly good enough for you." These ads are carefully lit with concealed spots. They never include any vulgar information about how many people actually read them or how many products they actually sell. They just hang there and are treated like so many Rembrandts in a museum.

But quiet and subtle isn't the Howard Marlboro style. What we show our clients and prospective clients now is what Jimmy Lee saw that afternoon — a set of testimonial letters from 75 Fortune 500 companies mixed with testimonials from an equal number of smaller companies. Most of these begin with "Dear Mike," and all of them include congratulations and thanks for a specific job our company has done for them. Next to the letter from a vice president of Pillsbury congratulating us for putting in a merchandising hardware system which now dominates the dairy cases in over 30,000 supermarkets around the country, is a letter from a small tofu health food outfit thanking us for delivering a test order of 500 meal planners under cost. Giant RJR Nabisco shares the wall with a small Florida drugstore chain.

As I led Jimmy Lee past these testimonials to our successes, hundreds of stories took shape in my mind. Behind each of those letters were weeks and months of grueling work, flashes of inspiration, a barrel of laughs and a couple of barrels of angry arguments. I got more out of that brief tour than the ambitious kid did. Reading those letters again, suddenly seeing them with his fresh enthusiasm, helped me to focus my thoughts and to rethink what my business career and my success were all about.

It is said that when a man is drowning, his entire life rolls out in front of him like a speeded-up movie. It was that way for me that late December afternoon. The sentences in those letters were like snapshots coming to life. But what struck me most vividly were the letters that weren't there, the near misses, the account resignations and firings, the failures which I am convinced contributed more to my personal growth and the growth of Howard Marlboro than did the many successful case histories spread out along our walls.

Jimmy Lee and I talked for an hour back in my office. The in-store photos he'd taken were as good as anything our professional Photo Audit people could come up with. They included a very imaginative set of what he called "time-lapse stills" — taken from the same angle every hour for a period of 12 hours — which clearly showed the powerful impact of a new promotion we were running for Pillsbury refrigerated cookie mixes. He did his homework on our company since the day I first met him when we were in Chicago on General Foods business. He learned from reading the trade press that Pillsbury was one of our clients.

Of the 20 or so ideas he showed me, we had already put most into place or had discarded them because they didn't work. A few of his notions were crazy and totally unworkable. But he did have two solid, imaginative ideas for checkout counter displays that were brand new to me. I got as excited about them as he was and wrote out a check to him for $1,000 on the spot.

On the surface, Jimmy Lee and I appeared to live in two totally different worlds. I with my chauffeured limousine ready to take me back to a comfortable Long Island home, Jimmy with a return Greyhound ticket to Chicago in his raincoat pocket. But in the few minutes I spoke with him in my office, I knew this eager, risk-taking kid was very much like me. How many times had I followed a hunch and taken the first morning flight from La Guardia or JFK to God knows where on the gamble that a sudden idea would begin a new business chapter.

Jimmy won his gamble that day. Besides the check, I put him in touch with a new Chicago client, a man I knew would give him a chance to learn retailing.

But there was something more we shared. Call it a hunger, an excitement, a drive. It came from deep within and was only incidentally connected with success in monetary terms. He had shown the desire and the guts to be the best.

Nerve, Guts, Chutzpah: Big Balls

Earlier in my career, I had hit one of those low points. The bankruptcy of several large clients had forced my own small company into bankruptcy. I was trying to start again from scratch. I had little money. But, I had guts.

I went to an auction run by people of, shall we say, less than desirable reputations. They weren't thieves, but I was reasonably certain they were loan sharks who had repossessed equipment from some of their unsuccessful "clients." The auctioneer was a wonderful character whom I shall call Mickey Finn. Mickey offered for sale a piece of equipment which was perfect for bending metal into displays. I wanted that equipment badly. With it I could see a way to get back on my feet.

I bid $48,000. The fact that I had virtually no money in my bank account was a minor drawback. When the auction was over, I waited until everyone else had paid for his purchase with cash or cashier's checks as is required at virtually every auction. Then I approached Mickey with my personal check.

"What's dat?" he asked.

"My personal check for $48,000," I answered.

"You know we don't accept no personal check at an auction."

I looked as crestfallen and humble as it was possible for me to look and continued, "Mr. Finn, I didn't realize you didn't take checks. I really need this equipment to fill a big order I just got. If you will take this check, I'll take the equipment out of here tonight so I can fill the order next week."

Mickey looked closely at me and then at his watch. To this day, I don't know whether he saw something in me or simply was late for dinner. Whatever the reason, he grunted, "O.K., get it outta here."

"Gee thanks, Mr. Finn. Oh, by the way, that machine is really worth about $120,000. Would you mind giving me a bill of sale for that amount?"

Mickey stopped in his tracks and took another look at me. This time I'm sure he saw something in me. He even cracked something which might generously be described as a smile. "Sure," he grunted, and wrote out the bill of sale.

Then as I turned to leave, I hollered over my shoulder. "Mr. Finn, could you hold that check for a few days? I need to transfer the funds to my account!" This time he laughed out loud.

Things moved fast after that. In a small New England town, I found an abandoned factory that was perfect for our kind of business. This town was desperate for new business and jobs, and I knew it. I visited the local bank which carried the mortgage on the abandoned plant.

I explained to the banker that I wanted to open a business which needed space such as he had. The banker, overjoyed at the prospect of bringing employment to the town, offered to rent the factory for $100 a month, about 5% of what that same facility would have cost in New York.

"Do you need anything else?" he asked, as I was about to leave.

"Well, now that you mention it, I could use some working capital."

"Do you have any collateral?" he asked, hopefully.

"Sure" I replied, "I have a $120,000 piece of equipment." With that, I grandly produced Mickey Finn's bogus bill of sale.

Within a matter of moments, he lent me $100,000 with Mickey's equipment as collateral. I deposited his check into my account, thereby covering the $48,000 check Mickey was holding. Then, I used the $52,000 difference as working capital to buy raw material and, of course, to hire employees to produce the orders I would shortly get.

The rest, as they say, is history — almost. About four years later, the "Great Plastic Shortage" hit America and devastated the display business. Everyone was running around like a blind dog in a butcher shop, trying to find plastic to fill orders. I was no different.

My search led me to a company in New England. I was sitting in the waiting room when the door opened. I glanced up, and who to my wondering eyes should appear but my old "friend" Mickey Finn. He recognized me instantly, although not by name. "Hey, you're the kid with the big balls," he announced to the whole waiting room.

"Mike Wahl," I corrected him.

"I hear things have been goin' great for ya," he continued.

"Yes," I answered, somewhat surprised that he'd kept track of me.

"Whaddya doin' here?" he asked. I explained about the plastic shortage. "Come with me," he ordered, and we marched straight into the president's office. Mickey took over. "This kid is a friend of mine. See that he gets what he wants." I was too surprised to say anything, but I waited as Mickey and the president had a whispered conversation. Mickey turned to me. "You get what you need with two conditions: you got to pay your bills in ten days, and you can't resell the plastic, you must use everything for your own account." I agreed instantly.

This "arrangement" worked great for us. We had plastic when some of our competitors had none. And needless to say, even though we could have resold our "allotment" for a handsome profit, we stuck to our bargain with Mickey.

Ethics: Know Your Honor Code

As I mentioned above, ethics are important to me and The Howard Marlboro Group. To understand why, you must understand the history and, to a lesser extent, the current state of the display business.

Historically, it has been a rotten business full of payoffs, bribery and cheating. One very well-known supplier in the industry leased over 20 cars for the personal use of purchasing managers at companies to which they were selling displays. This same company was notorious for padding bills to major U.S. corporations, then rebating the excess payment to the purchasing managers' personal bank accounts in one form or another. Paying college tuition bills for the purchasing managers' children was another favorite.

From the beginning, HMG took a blood oath that we would walk away from business rather than play this game. Our reasoning was simple. It's illegal and it's bad business — a real dynamite combination. We were convinced there were enough honest companies and honest people to build a decent business.

One day several years ago, one of the executives at Revlon came to our offices and met with my partner, Fred Howard, and me. He described the tremendous amount of business he wanted to give us and the opportunities which existed. The meeting ended with our saying it would be difficult for us to do business for two reasons: Cover Girl (Noxell) has been and continues to be our only client in the cosmetics business, and we have a policy against working for competing clients. Bottom line, we did not do business with them — ethics prevented it.

There is more to my concept of ethics than just obeying the law. I'm speaking of loyalty to employees and friends. Very early in my business life, I had an opportunity to experience and express this kind of loyalty.

Almost twenty years ago, I had a company called Wahl Associates. For me, no challenge was too big, no risk too great, and more importantly, the world was going only one way — up. We had experienced nothing called "a recession."

I had opened a chain of stores called "Cheap Mike's," had a display business, bought a paint company, bought a plastics distributing company and opened a real estate company, all with money I raised by going public in the late 1960's. We were borrowing heavily and leveraging everything we had to make acquisitions and fund our business during a rapid expansion. In that situation, everyone is your friend. However, interest rates were killing us, creating a difficult cash flow situation. I remember going to Chemical Bank and telling them that we should go Chapter 11. Their answer was, "Mike, relax. This will all blow over. The only thing you need is more money." They proceeded to lend me millions of additional dollars. Needless to say, they didn't want to write off the loan. I was supposed to believe that the more you owe, the better off you are.

To compound the problem, W.T. Grant, one of our largest customers, went bankrupt owing us $600,000 (in today's money, $2.5 million). Shortly thereafter, Mammoth Mart went bankrupt, and business became even tougher. I went to the bank again and told them that if we went Chapter 11 now, everyone could get paid off and we could reorganize the business. Once again, their answer was, "Mike, let's just condense the business a little bit," and they lent me more money. I finally went to the bank and told them the company had to go bankrupt, and I would not let them talk me out of it. Though we were a public company, I personally guaranteed about $8 million which is still an awful lot of money. I was worried about my reputation but even more worried about the employees and suppliers who had invested their faith in this organization.

Thanks to some great negotiating by Louis Nizer, one of the shrewdest attorneys of all time, we made a deal in which our suppliers were paid and our employees got two weeks' severance. I still smile when I think about employees receiving severance pay from a bankrupt company.

One other thing: I had run up a huge bill with my personal attorney, Jay Haft. I went to him and said, "I owe you $80 grand. It's gonna take me some time to pay you."

He answered, "Forget it, Mike. You don't owe me anything."

No one forgets a friend like that. His firm still represents me. The debt Jay so generously waived has been repaid many times in the years since.

Without the ethic of friendship and fair dealing, we would not have been able to start over with five employees and little backing and build the company that is today's Howard Marlboro Group.

Creativity: Stay Alert

Lots of intelligent people have spent their professional lives studying creativity and creative people. Anyone who can truly understand the creative process and bottle it will be the richest person on earth. HMG has won many awards for creativity in design and promotion. Clients and competitors often ask, "How did you think of that?" or "Where did you come up with that?"

One of our early successes is a good example. Pillsbury had developed a line of refrigerated doughs, an excellent product, but a nightmare to stock in the store. The tubular packages would tip over or roll around. The store clerks complained about the difficulty of stacking the product on the shelves. We even watched clerks trying to stack the product only to have it come rolling off the shelf onto the floor. Everyone instinctively realized that the lack of a shelf stacking system was seriously depressing sales.

In looking for ways to solve this problem, we stumbled across the answer, thanks to a process called the "Photo Audit." When we started in the display business, we developed the practice of taking pictures of displays or shelf conditions that caught our eye. We also took pictures of a product or a category to see how it looked in a representative sampling of different stores. This habit became a critical part of our creative, problem-and-solution process. As we reviewed our

Pillsbury photo audit, one grocer's shelves stood out. Upon closer inspection, we realized that someone (a stock boy, the store manager?) had gotten sick and tired of chasing the Pillsbury Dough Boy as he rolled off the shelf and into the aisle. Some enterprising retailer had constructed his own "shelf organizer" out of cardboard, cutting pieces and fitting them together in a way that made the packages easy to stock. You didn't have to be a rocket scientist to see that this jury-rigged system made life easier for both retailers and shoppers.

We took this idea, born of a retailer's desperation, and refined it into what we call "the organizer." In the last ten years, this simple device has found its way into virtually every supermarket in America and has stayed there. To me, it exemplifies the science of "space management." With the shopper's decision-making process (line of sight, data acquisition and sorting) in mind, we developed a simple mechanism that fits the shelf and organizes the product, thereby helping the consumer find what he or she wants.

This simple idea works. It arrested the decline of the refrigerated dough category and resulted in a major profit center for Pillsbury. It also generated over $12 million in sales for Howard Marlboro. Every time I see one in a supermarket, "the organizer" reminds me: space management works, photo audits work and good ideas come from the damnedest places.

Fire Island, for example, has been an intellectual "free fire" zone hospitable to artists, artisans and a large homosexual community for years. My wife and I used to visit in the summer to attend the art fairs and inhale the unique atmosphere pervading the place.

One evening, we stayed for dinner and found our way to a restaurant in the heart of the homosexual community. We were seated by a maitre d' dressed in an outrageous evening gown. His name was Richard. We looked around and saw the world as we had never seen it before. Everything in the restaurant had some visual trick or pun associated with it. The whole experience taught me to look more carefully at the most common article to see what made it different or charming.

As we walked back to the ferry, we stopped at a shop window. I saw a strange looking radio. I knew it was a radio because it had the letters R-A-D-I-O imprinted on it in a novel way.

"Wait a minute," I told my wife. "I'm going to get that radio." I bought the radio, took it to the office, removed the outside and hand-made a new outside with the letters P-I-N-C-H S-C-O-T-C-H in place of R-A-D-I-O.

Our client, Pinch Scotch, was instantly captivated by the radio. They wanted to give it away to all bartenders carrying their brand and ordered their standard premium quantity — 10,000! I had no way of manufacturing these radios, but I had a friend who was always bringing back exotic radios and the like from Asia. I called him, he contacted his friends in Hong Kong, and within a few months Pinch was carrying our radio into bars all over America.

These little radios started a whole new business for us — premiums. This eventually grew into our "Preferred Promotions" premium division, a multi-million dollar business that began with a little Pinch on Fire Island.

Since then, I've kept my eye out for unusual gizmos that catch the eye and charm you for unfathomable reasons. The logic is simple. If it catches my eye, it will catch the consumer's eye.

Another example of this creativity by serendipity occurred at the Copenhagen airport. I spotted a $10 sculpture of ultra-thin wires with silver balls attached that moved every time you shook it. It gave me an idea for a display. I bought it and took it home. By turning it upside down, it angled out like a Christmas tree. I made a prototype Christmas display for Johnny Walker scotch using colored balls on the sculpture I bought at the airport. It was well received, they placed a $500,000 order, and we ended up winning a Point-of-Purchase Advertising Institute Gold Award as "One of the Best Displays of the Year!"

Desire, nerve, ethics, creativity — that's what it took to build our business. That's what it takes to build any business.

PART II
The Rise of In-Store Marketing

CHAPTER THREE

Everything You Always Wanted to Know About Supermarkets

Over the last decade, New York has welcomed a new wave of Russian immigrants, many of whom have taken up the noble profession of cab driving.

In addition to the wisdom unique to New York cabbies, these Russian immigrants bring "the greatest gift that God can give us — to see ourselves as others see us." Whenever I identify a cabbie as a Russian immigrant, I always implore him to talk about life in Russia, why he came to America, Glasnost, etc.

Then I slip in the question: "When you first came to America, what impressed you the most?" I get the same answer every time — "the supermarkets."

One Russian told me enthusiastically about the first time he walked into an A&P on Long Island at 8 a.m. "Da shelves were full of everythink — apples, banaanaas, even, how you say, kiwi fruit. But nobody was een da store except da clerks. Not a single human beink. I thought, am I dreaming this? Is this appening? Have I died? In Russia, eef a store had that many thinks in it, the people would have mobbed eet because dey know eet would never be so full again een dair life."

"But een America," he went on, "everybody takes for granted the store will be full again tomorrow so nobody panics. That's when I realized how rich America was, when I went to that A&P."

Well, Ivan, you were right on two counts. A supermarket is a miracle, and we do take them for granted. In fact, they've become such a normal part of our lives that Americans hurry through them without stopping to understand what's going on or how this "miracle" works. The only time people talk about a supermarket is when something bad happens, or when they complain about prices. Americans don't realize that we spend far less of our disposable income on "food-at-home" than any other nation in the history of the world, despite the fact that supermarkets are very low margin businesses.

Misconceptions about the supermarket industry are much more widespread and fervently believed than is the truth. Because so much of our success at HMG is based on the cooperation and understanding we get from the supermarket industry, I feel I owe them something. I owe it to them to educate a small part of the public in the truth about supermarkets.

So, here is, "Everything You Always Wanted to Know About Supermarkets."

Basic Facts and Figures

Americans spend nearly $350 billion in 150,000 grocery outlets, but 12,000 large outlets account for almost 50% of that volume. Small convenience stores are over 33% of the total store count, but do only about 8% of the business.

Chain stores account for over 50% of the volume, but the independent sector is still enormous — doing approximately 45% of total volume across all store types.

The portion of Americans' disposable income spent at grocery stores continues to drop. As of 1970, we spent 13.0% of our disposable income on "food-at-home." By 1990, that number had dropped to 9.5%. In contrast, "food-away-from-home" continues its long-term growth. In 1990, 4.3% of Americans' disposable income was spent for "food-away-from-home," representing a nine-fold increase in such expenditures since 1965.

You have reason to feel overwhelmed at the breadth of choice in a supermarket. The typical chain supermarket stocks nearly 20,000 individual items known as SKU's (Stock-Keeping Units). This figure has doubled in the last decade, creating the grocer's dilemma. He's got more products than shelf space.

The grocer makes a different profit on each item. He sells more of certain types of items than others; therefore, some items contribute more to the grocer's profit. The table below provides a quick overview of the major categories sold in a grocery store (all numbers are taken from a *Progressive Grocer* study for 1988).

Category	% of Sales	% of Gross Profit	Gross Profit as a % of Retail Price
Food in packages	28.47	27.11	23.80
Perishable food	47.30	49.30	26.04
Non-food grocery	12.82	9.77	19.03
Health & beauty aids	4.04	4.09	25.28
General merchandise	4.38	6.21	35.44

This table requires some interpretation. Looking at the "food in packages" line, you can see that 28.47% of all the dollars spent in the store went for items in this category (canned goods, coffee, baby food, etc.). Moving across, you can see that this category contributed 27.11% of all the gross profit generated by the store. The last column is important to understand. It shows the percentage of profit made on a category. The grocer makes a 23.80% gross profit on food in packages. That means a canned item costing the consumer $1 has cost the retailer $.762, leaving him a gross profit of $.238 per can.

At this point, every grocer in America is screaming, "Tell them it's gross not net profit!"

An important distinction. Of the gross profit (which averages 24.99% for the whole store, or $.25 out of every sales dollar), the grocer must pay his staff, employee benefits, utilities, insurance and rent on the building, not to mention supplies (bags, cleaning supplies, etc.). In addition, the grocer must pay to advertise his products and pay interest on borrowed money to buy stock. Ideally, when he's done paying for all these things, he has something left which we call profit. Then he pays taxes on that. I'll tell you more later about net profit in the grocery business.

This next table shows the ten largest individual categories in the grocery store ranked on the basis of contribution to gross profit.

Category	% of Sales	% of Gross Profit	Gross Profit as a % of Retail Price
Meat	16.87	15.82	23.45
Produce	9.23	11.96	32.40
Dairy	8.19	7.80	23.78
Frozen foods	6.22	6.26	25.14
Soft drinks	3.93	4.31	27.42
Deli	2.40	3.44	35.81
Household supplies	3.49	3.23	23.19
Packaged bread	3.38	2.78	20.50
Beer and wine	2.99	2.77	23.15
Paper goods	3.77	1.68	17.44

As you can see, the meat department contributes over 15% of the total gross profit of the store. You may be surprised to learn that the grocer makes a lower profit margin on meat than on the average item (23.45% for meat vs. 24.99% for the average item). So the next time you are about to scream at your butcher because the price of steak is too high, remember that the store is probably making less on that steak than on most other items.

Two categories on the list above deserve special mention: produce and deli. These are two of the "hottest" categories in the store. Americans are buying more and more high-quality produce as a result of our national health kick. We're buying more and more at the deli to add variety to our menu and save time. The grocer is furiously promoting the deli as a way to strike back at his arch enemy, the restaurant, which over the years has stolen much of his food tonnage and profit.

The produce section is growing twice as fast as the total store — the deli at about half that rate. The real good news as far as the grocer is concerned is that produce and deli have relatively high gross margins, 32.4% and 35.8% respectively. So, here we have a real retailer's dream — big categories growing fast and commanding high margins.

Now for the bad news — both produce and deli have relatively high labor costs, so their real profit is significantly less than their gross profit percentage would suggest at first glance. Cost aside, however, grocers are really focusing on these categories. Go into a new supermarket in town and look at the space devoted to deli and produce. If you're a real grocery store freak, take a trip to Southern California and visit a Von's Pavilion, a supermarket designed to highlight produce. You actually enter a Pavilion store in the produce section. After ten steps, you find yourself surrounded by mountains of fruits and vegetables. The message is clear — Von's is serious about produce.

Von's is also serious about controlling costs. Most of that 25% gross profit margin is eaten away by operating costs. In fact, the average supermarket has only about $.015 of every sales dollar left after expenses are paid.

People are surprised to learn that labor is, by far, the supermarket's biggest cost. As one disbeliever remarked, "How can labor be that big a percentage when it's a self-service store?" Well, it's true the consumer does a significant share of the work in a supermarket, but there's still plenty of work for the stock boys, checkout clerks, produce manager and butchers. Nearly $.115 of every sales dollar goes for salaries and another $.03 for fringe benefits.

Store occupancy costs (rent and utilities) take up almost $.04 of every sales dollar, and the utility bill is almost as high as the rent. Supermarkets use an enormous amount of energy keeping things frozen and refrigerated. They were devastated during the energy crisis when utility rates went up. Grocers won't be caught napping again. They now use equipment which converts the hot air coming out of the freezers into energy to heat (or cool) the entire store. Chances are that your local grocery store is one of the more energy-efficient locations in your neighborhood.

New Profit and Cost Control

The average grocer takes about $.015 out of every sales dollar to the bank — that's right, $.015! Most grocers spend that much on advertising alone. Small wonder many chains have turned their ad departments into profit centers, and in the process, turned their merchandise buyers into sellers of ad space and transformed the manu-facturer's salesmen into buyers of ad space. It's a strange world!

With labor being such a large percentage of total store costs (about 68%), you can appreciate why grocers spend so much time figuring out staffing schedules. Before the advent of computerized software, some grocers spent hours counting traffic flows to optimize labor scheduling, putting on enough staff to keep customers happy but not enough to make the accountants unhappy. As you might expect, most of the store's labor is at the "front end," about 25% of which is the checkout clerk and another 15% the bag boy.

When you see these two costs, it's no longer a mystery why a Cub store, which has no baggers, has low prices, or why the industry is watching tests of a new computerized checkout stand where the cus-tomer checks herself out using an automatic scanner without a clerk. Don't laugh. You said you'd never pump your own gas, but now over 50% of gallonage is pumped by the consumer.

To ensure the maximum return on the labor dollar in such a low-margin, high-labor-cost business, supermarket executives look at sales six ways from Sunday. For example, they measure weekly sales per checkout lane ($24,821 for a chain store); weekly sales per employee ($3,584 for a chain); sales per employee hour ($92.91) and that old favorite, weekly sales per square foot of selling area ($8.31). These may seem like meaningless statistics to you, but trust me when I tell you that grown men and women spend years of their lives trying to make these numbers go up or down depending upon which way is good for business.

One way supermarkets reduce labor and increase profits is by jug-gling full-time and part-time employees. A typical supermarket employs twice as many people part-time as full-time. A large chain store will have nearly 100 employees, of whom only a little more than 33% are full-time.

Other carefully watched statistics are the number of transactions per week (12,000+ cash register rings in the average store, over 20,000 in a really big store), the average transaction size ($17 or so in a chain store) and the number of times per year the store sells the equivalent of its inventory (15 times for an average store, over 20 for a large, well-run store).

The reason management is concerned about inventory turns is pretty simple. The typical store has over $600,000 sitting on its shelves. No one wants to keep that many dollars lying around idle. Inventory turns and a related concern, shelf space allocation, will receive more attention over the next few years because grocery retailers are building larger and larger stores that will accommodate larger and larger inventories.

The driving force here is the time crunch Americans feel and the remedy they prescribe — one-stop shopping. Supermarket management is responding to the consumer by building larger stores that accommodate whole sections and types of merchandise previously available only in a drugstore, mass merchandiser, appliance store, card shop, florist shop, etc.

The Format Game

Supermarkets are picking and choosing among categories previously featured at other retailers, looking for those that offer high returns per foot of space (like flowers), or those that attract customers into the store (like pharmacies and banks). The objective here is to balance space yield with customer pulling power for maximum profit. In the supermarket business, this balancing act has a name — it's called the format game.

A lot of time and energy in the supermarket business is devoted to designing, testing and changing format. At last count, academicians had identified ten distinct grocery formats. The table below summarizes these formats and their differences.

The table gives a general idea of the differences between the formats: sheer size, item assortment and the percentage of non-food items (general merchandise and health and beauty aids). But the table doesn't reveal two things: which formats are "low service/low price" and which formats are going to "win."

The list contains five formats that can be called "low service/low price" formats — both warehouse formats, the hypermarket, the limited assortment store and the wholesale club. These formats save costs and pass on the savings to the consumer through a variety of strategies. They employ less help (i.e., no bag boys), no individual price marking, bare bones fixturing and, most controversially, different buying and stocking strategies.

Category	Total Area/ Sq. Ft.	Weekly Sales	# of Items	GM/HBC % of Sales
Conventional				
Supermarket	22,500	$ 138,000	15,000	8%
Superstore	42,000	290,000	23,000	13%
Food/Drug Combo	54,000	375,000	29,000	18%
Warehouse Store	43,000	215,000	14,500	6%
Super Warehouse	59,000	555,000	22,500	8%
Super Combo	95,000	950,000	60,000+	35%
Hypermarket	174,000	1,440,000	100,000+	40%
Limited Assortment	10,000	61,000	800	6%
Wholesale Club	105,000	970,000	5,000	65%
Convenience Store	2,500	11,300	3,400	7%
Other	NA*	18,500	NA*	NA*

* Not available due to the large number and varied sizes of these operations.

Some of these formats vary the product assortment according to what they can buy "on deal" from manufacturers. Others buy only commercial or industrial pack sizes. The limited assortment store stocks only generics, private label or "off brands." In one way or another, low price formats attempt to take advantage of manufacturer promotion and packaging practices to provide consumers with lower-cost merchandise.

With the exception of the unique convenience store format, all of the formats listed above are simply improvements on the supermarket format which was developed after World War II. They vary primarily in size and in the number of specialty departments. Some "Year 2000" stores now contain eat-in restaurants, Chinese food carryouts, on-premise sausage shops, pharmacies, full-service cosmetic counters, yogurt shops, juice bars, videotape rental and a home health care center.

Picking a winning format is neither quite as difficult nor as easy as it seems. The fact is that each format works somewhere and fails somewhere. However, it appears that the superstore and the food/drug combo formats are winners and will be with us into the

21st Century. The limited assortment store is a loser doomed to extinction by its fatal combination of low service, unknown brands and the need for the consumer to shop other outlets for complete satisfaction.

The hypermarket and wholesale club have been the subject of considerable study, partly because they are unique and have had a dramatic impact on shopping habits. The hypermarket, an American adaptation of a highly successful French invention, is a format which works well in limited numbers in most metropolitan areas. The amount of investment necessitates considerable research into a specific location, store design, etc. The format itself seems to have enough flexibility and appeal to find its way in the U.S., although some shoppers are repelled by the sheer size of the store, the length of time it takes to shop, crowding, driving distance, etc.

The wholesale club seems to be a clear winner because it combines the price appeal of wholesale with the shopping convenience of retail, and because it has cleverly focused on efficiently supplying the unmet needs of small and medium-size restaurants, retailers and businesses. Nearly half the volume in this format is done by individuals buying for a business rather than home consumption. Many convenience store operators buy carton cigarettes from a wholesale club rather than through a conventional distributor.

But wholesale clubs also do land office business with certain consumers as well. In California, where wholesale clubs are a well-developed distribution channel, people talk of waiting for over 30 minutes to get into a crowded wholesale club on Saturday mornings when many people are stocking up for the next few weeks. Some people report driving over 100 miles just to shop at a wholesale club!

The growth of the wholesale club is bad news for many manufacturers, because other format operators feel manufacturers discriminate against them in favor of the wholesale club. As they grow, other formats will take out their frustrations on the manufacturer for real and imagined slights. For their part, manufacturers will reach new heights of creativity, providing the wholesale clubs with what they want while claiming not to discriminate against conventional outlets.

This battle is serious. A successful wholesale club can decimate a nearby supermarket. The typical new supermarket costs about $80 per square foot to build and equip. The average new store is nearly 50,000 square feet; it costs nearly $4 million to build, exclusive of land costs (as much as $2 million in some places) and inventory costs — another $600,000. By the time the land is bought, the store built, fixtured and stocked, someone has a $6M to $7M investment. No wonder supermarket executives want protection from "unfair" competition.

Attracting and Keeping the Consumer

Once the store is open, grocers know they must meet a few threshold criteria or they will surely fail. Here's what consumers say are the ten most important criteria in their choice of a store:

1. Cleanliness
2. All prices labeled
3. Good produce department
4. Accurate, pleasant clerks
5. Low prices
6. Freshness date marked on products
7. Good meat department
8. Shelves usually kept well-stocked
9. Unit pricing signs on shelves
10. Convenient store location

Personally, I never get much nourishment out of lists like this because these factors seem obvious. Virtually every successful store operator measures up to these standards, yet we know that some stores are hugely successful because they have something extra.

There are two factors which make some stores special. The first is that they manage to instill a sense of ownership in the store customers. I'm not sure I know exactly how this is done, but I've listened to countless consumer interviews and heard people say, "It's my store ...," "I feel like I own it ...," "It's like I designed the store."

The other factor is the ability to instill a sense of familiarity in the customer that leads to a feeling of speed and efficiency in shopping — a sense of being in command or control.

26

Again, I'm not sure exactly what contributes to this feeling, but I've heard it expressed in many ways. "I just feel comfortable there." "Everything is so easy for me to find." "I don't feel crowded or rushed even when I'm in a hurry."

These two factors are obviously closely related. If I had one piece of advice for a store operator in the U.S., it would be this: "Make your customers feel as though they own the store!"

One reason this sense of command or familiarity is important is that it lends confidence to the consumer in her performance of a very complex process — shopping.

The typical consumer comes into a store with 20,000 choices, five of which are new every day. She scans more than 300 items per minute looking for items she knows she needs and looking for suggestions as to items she wants.

The consumer enters this marketplace virtually unarmed. Over two-thirds have no shopping list at all. Nine out of ten do not bother to check the store's circular for specials when they arrive. Eight out of ten bring no coupons.

With the exception of a few specific items which triggered the trip to the store and staples purchased virtually every trip, the majority of items purchased are purchased on impulse. Surprisingly, for example, 75% of oral hygiene sales are impulse.

We at HMG are in business because consumers **do** buy on impulse, and we are experts at helping them do so.

The harried consumer completes her trip through the store in 45 minutes. The average shopping trip time has dropped in the last decade, putting more pressure on the store operator to keep the consumer moving and more pressure on manufacturers to make their products more visible to the shopper on the fly.

At HMG, we believe more money is going to be spent at the point of sale on advertising, couponing, merchandising and displays. We think more money will be diverted from conventional ad media into new, "unconventional," retail-based media. We believe the store of the future will be full of advertisements creating awareness and desire just a few feet from where awareness and desire will be transformed into a purchase.

Who's the Best?

As I finish this chapter about everything you always wanted to know about the great American grocery store, it occurs to me that you might want to know what store or chain I believe is the best in the U.S.

Right out of the box, let me say there's no accurate answer to that question. Every major chain in the U.S. has a few new stores that are magnificent. And there are numerous single-store, independent outlets which command the affection and the dollars of their customers.

But if you absolutely forced me into a corner, I'd have to say that of the regional chains I've seen, Albertsons seems to have consistently high quality outlets. Among local chains, I find Byerly's of Minneapolis to be beautiful stores. But the single most memorable store I ever saw was in Ft. Wayne, Indiana, of all places. It was called Everys. It's been nearly thirty years since I saw that store, but I remember it like it was yesterday. It looked like a giant circus tent, and it had a huge coffee roaster and grinder in the center of the store. The entire place smelled of freshly ground coffee. It smelled like a home and looked like a carnival.

God, I loved that store!

I felt like I owned it. It gave me such a feeling of confidence and command.

CHAPTER FOUR
The Decline of Advertising

When I started in business, the advertising man was a glamorous and powerful figure in our society. Movies, and books like "The Man in the Gray Flannel Suit," made him seem larger than life — shrewd, creative, sophisticated and influential.

Every night, millions of Americans spent hours in front of the TV watching and, more importantly, being affected by his handiwork. Detractors called him a huckster, but no epithet really stuck. His touch was unavoidable, his influence undeniable.

Some critics questioned the social utility, the motives, even the morals of advertising. The most widely read of these assaults was Vance Packard's "The Hidden Persuaders," which chastised the industry for diverting society's attention and perverting its more generous instincts.

Packard's criticisms were never fully accepted by society. People simply didn't believe they could be sold something they didn't need. In fact, most Americans would have agreed with the president of Procter & Gamble, the nation's largest advertiser, who said, "The best way to kill a bad product is to advertise it so that more people try it and find out firsthand just how bad it really is."

Other defenders of business, advertising and "The American Way" pointed out that the ability to advertise is a powerful incentive to invent new products and improve old ones.

In the early 1970's, advertising reached the zenith of its effectiveness. Politicians discovered its principles could be adopted for their purposes. Ad men became advisers on election tactics, even policy — Bob Haldeman, Ron Ziegler and Dwight Chapin were all advertising executives before they were politicians. Individual ad campaigns and snappy slogans were incorporated into the nation's vocabulary.

My, how times have changed.

Since that high point in the early 1970's, the advertising industry has been in a state of relative decline. In 1988, a much discussed study by Information Resources, Inc., a Chicago-based research company, stunned the ad industry by "proving" that much advertising was ineffective. This wasn't a complete surprise to the marketing community which had been allocating ever-increasing expenditures to promotion rather than advertising for years before the benchmark study.

The oldest major advertising medium, newspapers, has been weakened by declining subscriptions and a less literate reader; a newer medium, television, has seen its power diluted by technology and greed.

Technology has weakened television by changing the balance of power from broadcaster monopoly to viewer choice. Up until the 1980's, the American viewer could watch any show he wanted, provided it came in vanilla, chocolate or strawberry (NBC, CBS or ABC). By the end of the 1980's, more than half of all Americans were wired for cable, with its seemingly infinite choices. By 1989, 70% of U.S. homes were equipped with video cassette recorders, allowing users to take command of their valuable viewing hours. Cable and the VCR have meant that less than 70% of viewing time is spent with the three basic flavors of NBC, CBS and ABC. Daytime television, once one of the most powerful and efficient of all advertising alternatives, has degenerated into a medium watched by toddlers, retirees and the unemployed.

As viewership waned, prices waxed. In what must rank as one of the greatest acts of piracy in the 20th Century, the price of air time for advertising increased as audiences dropped. The cost-per-thousand-viewers, the standard measure of advertising efficiency, outpaced inflation in every year of the 1980's.

In 1980, a typical 30-second spot on nighttime network TV cost $57,900 and delivered a thousand viewers for $4.80. In 1990, that same 30-second spot cost $122,200 and delivered viewers at $10 per thousand.

This cost escalation would not have hurt marketers if the worth of the customer had increased proportionately to the increase in advertising costs. This was not the case, however. Mass marketers were fighting for smaller and smaller segments (some would say fragments) of markets, and the basic marketing equation was thrown out of balance. As the cost of reaching and converting the relatively few new users of a fragmented category grew too great to justify the expense, marketers compensated in several ways.

First, they leveraged existing brand names into multiple flavors and fragrances, or whole new categories. The Velveeta cheese brand name went on a line of dry packaged dinners; the Jello brand name went on pudding pops, and the Coke brand got a new first name, Diet, all because marketers realized it was cheaper to rely upon the historical power of the brand name than the current power of television advertising. The effect was to allow marketers to amortize the cost of advertising — single brand inventory over several different products.

Secondly, marketers compensated for escalating TV costs by moving to shorter message lengths. One-minute commercials, which were the standard message length as recently as 1965, became :30's, and now :30's are becoming :15's. The net result is more commercial clutter and less effective commercials. You might say that more is less.

The simplest way to measure the decline in a commercial's effectiveness is through "recall" scores, i.e., the percentage of people who remember something meaningful about a commercial the day after it has been seen. For a decade, these scores have been declining. One must conclude that either viewers are dumber, commercials are poorer or, most likely, clutter is overwhelming the viewer's ability to focus on a message.

Today, advertisers are paying more and more to show a shorter and shorter selling message to fewer and fewer and less attentive viewers.

I can only imagine what would have happened if I'd gone to my friends in Winston-Salem and told them that in ten years, I would cut the L'eggs fixture size in half, double our price, guarantee that fewer people would walk past it and that fewer still would take note of it. I know the L'eggs folks would have begun looking for other ways to spend their money, and that's one of the main reasons marketers have

31

been shifting their expenditures away from advertising and toward promotions and in-store displays.

We have not yet seen the bottom of the decline in the effectiveness of television advertising. As commercial lengths shorten, copywriters have less time to romance the difference between products at a time when these differences are ever more subtle. As a result, copywriters are forced to fall back on fluff and puff, weasel words and witticisms instead of the simple virtue of product difference and (hold your breath) product superiority. As commercial lengths decline to 15 seconds and effectiveness declines with it, where is the manufacturer's incentive to improve? Will any copywriter ever again get to use that magic word "better?"

One group which has fully realized the implications of these trends is Wall Street. They understand that as advertising loses its effect as an agent of change, current branded positions become more valuable. They realize that as retailers increase in strength and marginal brands wither, major brands become proportionately stronger. There are major implications here for stock prices, acquisition and divestiture values of whole companies.

However, one monumental rainbow is appearing faintly in the sky — interactive TV. Patents have recently been issued for a simple system that would allow every home in America to interact with TV in real time, playing "Wheel of Fortune" and matching wits with Dan Marino or Sparky Anderson.

This technology can alert you to a special show, commercial or buying opportunity of pre-declared interest to you. It might just reinvigorate TV and give marketers a new weapon in the war to win the hearts and minds of consumers.

In the meantime, as marketers continually re-evaluate the weapons currently available, the shift toward in-store marketing goes on.

Part II

CHAPTER FIVE
The Rise of the Retailer

Any manufacturer who completes an accurate Future's Audit (see Chapter Seventeen) will conclude that the retailer is growing in power. The clearest evidence of this is the shift in marketing expenditures toward pure trade promotion spending.

If companies accurately accounted for every "marketing" expenditure (including in-store displays, retail ad allowances, salesforce time, etc.), they would discover that more than half of all marketing dollars are spent to influence the retailer — trying to persuade him to stock a new product or size, keep a product in stock, increase its shelf space, lower the shelf price, feature it in an ad or display it off-shelf.

The situation has not progressed in the U.S. to the extent that it has in Europe, where at each year's end, retailers inform manufacturers that the price of staying on-shelf during the next year is a payment equal to X% of last year's sales. The growing ownership of American retailers by foreigners, especially Europeans, suggests that it won't be long before this repugnant practice will be introduced into the U.S. retailing bloodstream.

Two questions need to be asked: Why is the retailer rising in power? What does it mean to American manufacturers?

The Retailer's Rise in Power

The increasing power of the retailer is the result of a combination of trends that are weakening the traditional ability of manufacturers to control their direct influence on the consumer and actions taken by retailers themselves to improve the way they do business.

Against the Manufacturer

The two main trends working hand in hand against the manufacturer are the decline of the power of advertising and the fragmentation of the mass consumer market. I discussed the advertising situation in the previous chapter. What's happening with the consumer is that we have gone from mass-marketing to micro-marketing. Our "mass-marketing system," which depended upon the validity of mass-market research and which worked for decades, doesn't work anymore. It's becoming trickier and more difficult to predict consumer behavior on the basis of membership in large demographic groups. (Knowing that an individual is a white Anglo-Saxon male Protestant, age 18 to 34, tells us infinitely less about his lifestyle and brand preferences in 1991 than it did in 1971. Today's consumer is choosing from a wider range of options in living, thinking and buying because he's aligning himself with different cultural, religious and even age groups depending upon where and with whom he lives, what kind of job he holds, his hobbies, etc.)

With spending power in the hands of working mothers, boomers, busters, teens, yuppies and countless ethnic groups, to name a few of the more well-known demographic blips that are coming and going across the marketing radar screen, the old easy-to-please mass market has been fragmented into scores, maybe hundreds, of smaller markets. The retailer is no longer just a conduit for product to a consumer pre-sold by inexpensive TV advertising. In most cases, he is now critical to the success of the manufacturer's communication process, and he knows it.

For the Retailer

For years, supermarket retailers earned a return on their equity that was less than they could have earned putting this money in CD's at the neighborhood bank. No business can survive if it doesn't earn money greater than the cost of capital. It was inevitable that retailers would smarten up, and three key trends are the result:

- Better trained management personnel
- Improved information systems
- A consolidation of retailing to fewer, bigger stores

Over the past decade, no industry has improved the quality of its management as much as retailing. For years, the gap between the quality of manufacturing management and that of retailing had been startling, even embarrassing, especially at the middle and upper middle levels. A standing joke was that if you wanted to pick out a supermarket buyer at a convention, you simply looked for the guy with fingers missing. The implication was that he was someone who had started as a produce boy or as a butcher's assistant, lost a finger to an errant meat cleaver but stayed in the business, often foregoing college or any formal business training outside of the store.

This unflattering parody had a grain of truth to it. When a friend interviewed the director of advertising of the second largest supermarket in America and asked, "What is your advertising strategy?" — he expected to hear a learned discussion about target customers, customer attitudes, the shopping experience, bonding, etc.

Instead, the advertising V.P. answered, "We have a strategy like a pyramid."

"A pyramidal strategy?" my friend offered.

"Yes, that's it, a pyramidal strategy."

My friend thought that he was the victim of a joke, but pressed on. "What's a pyramidal strategy?"

"Well," said the V.P., drawing a triangle on a piece of paper, "we put a few of the hottest-priced items on top, a few more hot-priced items on the next few rows and lots of other items here at the bottom, and this forms a pyramid. That's our strategy."

My friend insists that this incredible scene took place without any recognition by the V.P. of other factors which might contribute to a genuine strategy. I believe him.

Retailers have indeed suffered because of unsophisticated personnel, especially at the critical buyer/merchandiser level. Happily, the quality and education levels of their personnel have improved dramatically in the past decade, helped by another major development — the rapid increase in marketing data, especially from scanners.

As a V.P. of sales at Procter & Gamble once said, "Retailers now know more than we [manufacturers] do, and they know it sooner." Any major retailer can now rapidly measure the effect of critical marketing decisions. For example, without extraordinary effort, a retailer can ascertain:

- what the best combination of brands and sizes is in a category.

- what the effect of special deals is on movement and profit in a category.

- what the impact of off-shelf display is in various categories and brands.

With a little more time and effort, he can measure the effect of various combinations of advertising, feature items, special service departments and store layout on store traffic, sales volume and gross margin. To supplement their efforts, retailers can now call on a host of external experts and consultants capable of juggling data that can project the impact of X, Y, Z action.

The point is that this knowledge is power, and the knowledge balance is tilting more and more toward the retailer.

This is also the case with the balance of consumer traffic. More and more consumers are concentrated in fewer and fewer retail outlets. From 1980 to 1990, the total number of grocery stores decreased from 167,100 to 145,000, while the number of stores with sales greater than $2,000,000 grew from 27,080 to 30,750. These stores accounted for 71% of sales in 1980 and 74% in 1989, representing a substantial increase in concentration. Furthermore, there is evidence to suggest that consumers are more loyal to their retail store than to popular brands. For example, about 50% of all supermarket customers shop regularly at only one store, a loyalty level enjoyed by few brands.

With consumers shopping regularly at fewer, bigger outlets, manufacturers are being forced to compete for shelf space and merchandising attention or risk serious harm in the marketplace.

We have a client with a small division selling high-quality, deli-style processed meats. The products are regional favorites throughout the West, especially in California. At present, there are over 1,000 Class A supermarkets in California, but one small chain with 12 huge stores is this company's fourth largest customer in all of California, even though they stock only two of the 30 products the company makes. Imagine the clout this customer has when he asks for a favor or some form of special treatment!

It's no wonder the power of huge retailers grows, despite the Robinson-Patman Act which requires manufacturers to provide equal and proportionate treatment to all trade retailers. Large retailers still receive special treatment, and because they do, their customers benefit. They keep coming back, thus rendering the larger retailer ever stronger.

Implications for the Manufacturer

What does this mean for the manufacturer? On one level, it probably means that more of the available profit in any given transaction will go to the retailer, thereby cutting the margins and profits of the manufacturer. More time, effort and money will be spent on the retailer — on in-store effort and in-store fixturing.

Something else is going to happen as well. I think manufacturers are going to get closer to retailers. When our manufacturing clients ask us about the future, we tell them to get as close to the retailer today as they tried to get to the consumer yesterday. We tell them to bond with the retailer, to become his partner, to focus on what's called the "Chain of Value" and to help the retailer build it.

Building the "Chain of Value" will be one of the major developments in American business in the 1990's. It will only occur, however, if manufacturers and retailers work together. If they do, everybody will win, especially consumers.

What is the "Chain of Value?" It's every decision and action by manufacturer and retailer that affects the cost of the product and its appeal to the consumer. Manufacturing and marketing a product involves policies and practices that can increase the cost of doing business without really improving the end result; for example:

- promotion practices that increase handling and billing.

- shipping containers that can't be stored or handled in a warehouse.

- display material that doesn't fit on shelves.

- packages enlarged beyond all reason.

For too long, the manufacturer and the retailer have thought of each other as adversaries or, at best, as in-laws who did not really like one another but had to tolerate each other for the sake of the children — in this case, the consumers.

Building the "Chain of Value" requires manufacturer and retailer to recognize that serving the consumer is in their mutual interest. It requires them to sit together and start from the very beginning examining every action they take and its effect on cost and value. With this laborious examination of every link in the "Chain ...," costs can be reduced, prices lowered, customers rewarded and profits raised.

Few retailers and fewer manufacturers are focusing on the "Chain of Value" today the way they will have to tomorrow. But it's coming.

And so are other developments. Within our shopping lifetime, we will see in virtually every corner of the U.S.:

- electronic, in-store couponing targeted to a specific consumer based upon her usage habits.

- "frequent buyer" cards that record a consumer's purchases, thereby facilitating promotions which reward purchase continuity, as well as other targeted promotion efforts.

- interactive, in-store devices designed to provide information and sell to the consumer at the point of sale.

- an electronically-integrated store connecting retail locations, wholesale warehouses, manufacturers, financial institutions and other service suppliers.

Each of these activities, thought to be impractical pipe dreams less than a decade ago, is available in the marketplace today.

For example, there is already a checkout lane electronic-couponing service operating in many supermarkets.

Procter & Gamble is in a joint venture with Donnelly and Check Robot to develop and test a frequent buyer card. This is an inventive, courageous and extremely expensive way of redressing the information imbalance between retailer and manufacturer. P & G wants to regain some control over information at the point of sale, thereby retaining some contact with and control over its consumers.

MarkitStar, a company I helped found, developed the first consumer interactive point-of-sale device in broad-scale use. This ground-breaking, shelf-edge computer system was placed in 30,000 drug and food stores by Noxell as part of its extraordinarily successful introduction of the Clarion cosmetic line. Other companies are working with MarkitStar to develop devices to supply information at the point of sale where the shortage of trained personnel has made the human touch virtually non-existent in mass retailing.

All this may sound like we are entering the golden age of retailing in which a large percentage of the total available profit in a transaction shifts from manufacturer to retailer, thereby dramatically improving the retailer's financial prospects. Unfortunately for the retailer, this is not completely true.

Although some redress of the imbalance has occurred and more will occur, retailers have their own set of problems that will keep them from ever realizing the returns manufacturers enjoy.

One is their dependence upon a shrinking supply of cheap, relatively unskilled labor, the shortage of which computerization is designed to replace. However, chances are computerization won't be able to replace labor fast enough to compensate for the need to increase salaries in order to attract competent help.

Ironically, as retailers, especially food retailers, are seeking ways to reduce labor by computerizing some operations, they are also adding high cost, service-intensive sections. Just as the labor supply is shrinking and salaries must inevitably escalate, retailers find themselves adding in-store bakeries, service delis, sit-down restaurants, sausage shops, etc.

Why? Well, this gets to the heart of the problem of retailing itself — the inability to differentiate and realize a "value added" margin. Because service businesses like retailing cannot patent themselves or protect a proprietary advantage for more than a nanosecond, they ultimately offer consumers only minimal differentiation to justify a larger margin. Adding services like delis and bakeries is a way of establishing a competitive difference, but they seldom represent a "sustainable, competitive advantage." Consequently, retailers ultimately compete on price and location, two thin reeds on which to erect a highly profitable business.

Nevertheless, we have entered the age wherein retailers and manufacturers must form partnerships, and where possible, build together a new "Chain of Value" to attract and keep customers. In this new era, marketing to the retailer will be almost as important as marketing to the consumer.

CHAPTER SIX
Partners in Profit

From the day we first opened our doors, we've always considered HMG sort of a commercial marriage broker, forging a partnership between retailer and manufacturer at the point of sale. The way we saw it, our displays helped both the retailer and the manufacturer make money by making it easier for the consumer to find the product he or she wanted.

We have developed a healthy respect for the skills of the manufacturer and the experience of the retailer. We've cultivated close communications with retailers, particularly regarding the major merchandising, promotional and marketing issues facing our manufacturing clients. All the while, we've been aware of the cool, correct, sometimes even adversarial relationship between manufacturer and retailer. Now it would appear that some manufacturers and retailers are exploring a new kind of relationship. The common name for this uncommon relationship is "retail partnering."

The essence of retail partnerships is a change from periodic, transaction-oriented contact in an "I sell/you buy" atmosphere, to more intense, continuous contact in a cooperative "I win/you win" atmosphere.

The retailer/manufacturer dynamic has common objectives:

- to drive out excess costs.
- to share knowledge.
- to meet consumers' needs.

- to increase the value to the consumer.
- to increase our respective profits.

If these objectives sound like Chevrolet, apple pie, baseball and the flag, please consider the level to which manufacturer/retailer relations had sunk. Historically, manufacturers regarded retailers with something between indifference and contempt. Their relationship was shaped by infrequent contact by low-level functionaries in a zero-sum transaction. Each one sought to justify his existence by returning to his boss with a bigger share of the transactional pie. Cooperation consisted of delivering the goods to the agreed point on the agreed day and receiving the agreed-upon check. Confrontation was the order of the day. Each party developed practices to help it win the game. The long-term implications of these practices on the overall cost of the transaction were lost in the short-term struggle for advantage.

As competition among manufacturers intensified and retailers grew in strength, many manufacturers (and a few retailers) began to question the nature of their traditional relationship and its effect on profitability.

Those seeking a model for a new relationship found examples far and near. They examined the relationship between Japanese automakers and their suppliers. The suppliers help manufacturers in providing exceptional service levels (just-in-time parts delivery, for instance) and by reducing rework levels via zero defect supply policies. In this relationship, everybody wins. The consumer gets a superior product at a low price, the manufacturer sells lots of cars at a manufacturing cost below Detroit's and the parts manufacturers sell lots of parts. (It is one of the great ironies of history that this "Japanese system" was pioneered by an American, Dr. W. Edwards Deming.)

Ironically, another model came from the experience of manufacturers and grocery retailers while developing local and regional marketing promotion efforts. These efforts not only involved an investment of manufacturer dollars, but also required collaboration between executives at a level above the standard salesman/buyer. These promotions required manufacturer and retailer to share information, to reinforce one another's efforts and — wonder of wonders — to work for a common goal defined roughly as "maximum, mutual profitability." However, these romances were temporary, leaving the basic, transactional relationship unchanged.

Commercial historians date the shift toward "partnership" with Campbell's shift from a brand-driven salesforce to an account-driven salesforce in the mid-1980's. But for my money, the experiment began in earnest when Procter & Gamble moved a fully staffed account team to Bentonville, Arkansas, the headquarters of its largest customer, Wal-Mart.

Sam Walton has said publicly that "Wal-Mart and P&G are writing the next chapter of manufacturer/retailer relations," but to the outside world, this relationship has been shrouded in secrecy, myth and rumor. Periodic press releases and articles permit careful observers to piece together the nature of the "partnership," but a clearer picture emerges from a series of speeches by Lew Pritchett, the recently retired V.P. of sales at P&G and the principal instigator of the extraordinary P&G/Wal-Mart experiment.

In speeches notable for their attempt to keep inside information confidential, the colorful and charismatic Pritchett draws together the disparate public reports into a comprehensive scenario in which P&G is attempting to integrate with retailers the workings of its external operation in order to reduce costs and improve mutual marketing effectiveness.

Into this "new partnership," the manufacturer contributes brand franchises, in-depth knowledge of consumer category dynamics, control of external logistics, research capability, knowledge of its strategic objectives and money while the retailer supplies control of the retail environment, market-specific scanner data, knowledge of internal logistics, knowledge of chain marketing objectives and, again, money.

One of the major ironies in this situation is that it is P&G which led the experiment with retail partnering. This company has spent literally billions of dollars to create and maintain branded consumer franchises impervious to trade machinations. For years, the company adopted an attitude of almost Olympian indifference to its retail customers. In a conversion unrivaled since that of St. Paul two millennia ago, the trade's "persecutor" becomes its "partner."

The irony is not restricted to P&G's side of the equation. Many retailers have abandoned any pretense at collaboration with suppliers. They pit one against the other to force purchase prices to the lowest possible level.

The trade partnering being tested by P&G and Wal-Mart requires mutual trust in order to move from a short-term, adversarial mentality to a long-term, cooperative partnership. Such a scheme is grounded in the possibility of increased profits. Where are the profits to be found?

There are clues. Increased profits are available from identifying excess costs built into the old business system and then aggressively driving out those costs. This is the "Chain of Value" concept discussed in the previous chapter. Second, increased profits are also available from improved, collaborative marketing that increases both parties' share of the market.

Let's examine these theoretical profit sources. It is easy to believe that two entities with separate operating policies and procedures would invent practices which cost each other money. Promotional practices are a good example. P&G promoted its brands periodically. This could involve producing special packs at reduced line speeds, taking and processing special orders, etc. P&G had built a cost into its system for purposes it found justifiable. But from Wal-Mart's perspective, P&G's promotional practices simply increased the cost of doing business by introducing the costs of periodic, increased inventories, increased handling, order processing, etc.

When both sides stepped back and looked at their business systems, it became obvious that their lack of collaboration was costing everyone money. Then somebody introduced the novel idea that these two giants could pretend they were owned by the same person (the mythical consumer) and align their organizations so that this owner/consumer got the best possible deal.

Once this attitude was in place, all sorts of cost savings could be realized. P&G salesmen could stop writing orders, leaving that to computers and the logistical departments of both organizations. The P&G credit department could stop the absurd practice of checking Wal-Mart's credit on every order. For its part, Wal-Mart could agree to accept deliveries on a regular basis so that production and shipping schedules could be normalized.

On the profit increase side of the equation, collaboration offered a number of possibilities. A simple one to understand is increasing in-stock presence in key categories like diapers. This fast-turning, high-cubage, multiple-style category is particularly difficult to keep in stock, so any logistical improvements that reduce out-of-stocks would translate into increased sales for both P&G and Wal-Mart.

The jury is still out on the trade partnering "experiment" exemplified by the P&G/Wal-Mart "marriage." On the positive side, the new relationship has dramatically increased the number and nature of contacts between manufacturer and retailer. More functionaries know more about the workings of their retail or manufacturing counterparts than ever before. Both sides are more sensitive to each other's cost structures and marketing strengths.

Certainly, the mirror-image teams put in place by manufacturer and retailer are getting a training/learning experience that will make them vastly more valuable to themselves and to their respective employers.

Oddly enough, in the long run, the most lasting effect of retail partnering may take place not in the field at the point of contact, but back in the manufacturer's organization which is being, or has been, transformed so that it more closely mirrors the retailers' perceptions of an appropriate management structure, i.e., one dominated by category thinking, not brand thinking.

Internally, P&G's functional category management structure aligns almost perfectly with the way their field organization aligns externally with Wal-Mart's team. In principle, this means that a Wal-Mart warehouseman could call his counterpart on the category team in Cincinnati and get a reasonably quick answer to his problems — an organizational impossibility five years ago.

Skeptics of trade partnering abound. They argue that the organizational infrastructure it requires is too expensive for any but the largest manufacturers and retailers. The argument is as follows: Procter &

Gamble has enough volume going through Wal-Mart, and Wal-Mart buys enough goods from Procter & Gamble to justify special staffing. But the Jones Widget Company isn't big enough to put a special staff anywhere, even in Bentonville. Even large retailers can't assign a special team to every category, much less every supplier in every category.

I think this argument makes sense, which is why P&G and some other large manufacturers are probably attracted to the idea. Only a few large manufacturers can practice an aggressive trade alignment strategy, and to the extent that this is true, the larger, multi-category, multi-brand companies will benefit competitively from the strategy.

This raises another criticism made by some — trade partnering, they say, is illegal. According to them, it violates the Robinson-Patman Act requiring "equal and proportionate" treatment of all retailers. I have no specific knowledge whatsoever of P&G's efforts to protect themselves from this criticism, but I will bet next year's profits that this issue is receiving wall-to-wall coverage by P&G's legal department and top management. That's because someone, somewhere, sometime, is bound to sue P&G over trade practices of this kind. I want to make it clear that I have no knowledge or opinion regarding the validity of such a case, only that with the excess of attorneys we have in our society, one of them will persuade some allegedly aggrieved party to file suit.

Other skeptics cite the disintegrating power of brand franchises and the growing power of the retailer as working against a stable, long-term partnership. They argue that no differences exist among leading brands in most categories. In this environment, the consumer makes her judgement on the basis of price alone; therefore, the retailer makes his judgement on the basis of cost alone. According to this argument, a partnership with a manufacturer is meaningless, even ludicrous. What counts is price. The manufacturer with the best deal wins.

Ironically, P&G, which believes in the existence and value of differentiated brands, might well accept the premise that brand loyalty is eroding and turn that into a reason to do trade partnering.

Their sales pitch would go like this: "Mr. Retailer, if you really believe there is no difference among brands, why not team up with someone who can give you good prices and an array of superior services you can't get elsewhere?" In this scenario, P&G differentiates itself with superior service rather than superior products. What drives P&G's reasoning? The conviction that some form of partnering is advantageous to both retailer and manufacturer; that if any manufacturer is going to partner with major retailers, it will be P&G which will reap the advantage, not one of their competitors.

Stepping back for a moment from this ever-evolving issue, two thoughts come to mind.

First, this entire situation is being driven by the remarkable explosion in data availability and manipulation. This enables everyone to understand everyone else's management decision processes and systems.

Second, even in the most ideal trade partnering scenario, neither manufacturer nor retailer is really an expert in the art and science of point-of-sale presentation. I say this with some conviction and comfort because it means we at HMG can continue to play the role we have played for so long, that of uniting the interests of manufacturer, retailer and consumer at the point of sale.

CHAPTER SEVEN
The Heartbreak of Promotions

Go **For It, America**. That's what we called a promotion we devised for British Airways a few years ago. I almost used it as the heading for this chapter on promotions because it encapsulates the spirit of every promotion done every day by every manufacturer and retailer. They want you to

Go For It, America!

If that's a good metaphor for promotions, the Sunday paper is a good laboratory for understanding this exciting, expensive and often exasperating aspect of marketing.

One Sunday, I counted all the direct cents-off offers delivered to our house in the paper. It turned out my $1.50 Sunday paper was really worth about $20 in immediate, direct cash reductions if I were willing to buy the 75 products that offered these incentives.

If you had the patience to collect various proofs of purchase and then wait for the redemption check, you could save another $30, not counting major rebates on small appliances and automobiles.

That means one Sunday paper carried over $50 worth of bona fide cash offers.

This same exercise is repeated Sunday after Sunday in virtually every newspaper in America. If you multiply $50 x 52 Sundays x 60 million Sunday subscribers, you get $156 billion in potential redemption liability. Now you have some sense of what marketers are willing to spend to get you to buy their products.

Several points should be made immediately. Only a very small percentage of the offers made in the newspaper are ever redeemed (probably about 3%). But these redemptions are only a small percentage of the total monies spent by marketers. Promotion expenditures of all kinds account for at least two-thirds of all monies spent to influence a sale, of which about half is spent against consumers as opposed to retailers.

Now, I bet you're waiting for me to tell you all this money is well spent.

You're going to be waiting a long time. For reasons I'll explain in a moment, most of this money is spent with only the vaguest of evidence of what its impact will be in the marketplace.

Why then have marketers been spending all this money? The best answers aren't really very satisfactory, but here they are:

- Marketers have a religious faith that promotions do work.

- Doing a promotion often makes more sense and is always more emotionally satisfying than the next best alternative, which is to do nothing while your competition promotes like hell.

Just so you know where I'm coming from, I share this religious belief in promotions. I'm convinced they sell extra merchandise. One reason I'm convinced is that promotions often stimulate the company's salesforce to lean on the trade for more in-store display activity and I <u>know</u> that works.

More seriously, it's been extremely difficult to demonstrate exactly how effective most promotions really are in moving extra merchandise, that is, merchandise that would not have been purchased anyway by loyal consumers. Over the long haul, most companies have developed formulas enabling them to establish "cost per extra case moved" or "cost per new trier."

But let's return to the basic issue of why marketers run promotions. They want to sell more merchandise, but from a strategic sense, a marketer usually has a more narrow, focused reason to promote. In fact, he usually has one of three objectives:

- to generate trial of the product among new or infrequent users.

- to load regular customers with an abnormally large purchase.

- to induce continuity of purchases among casual or infrequent users.

Go for the most difficult task, which is to get consumers to try a product, especially a food product. That's why marketers spend so much money on activities like sampling and couponing. These are the two best ways to get a new consumer to try a product.

Sampling is pretty simple to understand, especially sampling of a new product. By definition, no one has tried the product, so the most effective (but expensive) way to generate trial is to give the product away. Usually, this is done through the mail, in the store or door-to-door.

It's pretty easy to figure out whether sampling is a good idea or not. You calculate the cost-per-thousand samples and then measure whether the thousand samples have generated an acceptable level of repeat purchases over a given period.

Coupons are a more complex issue:

- A lot of people don't redeem coupons at all.

- A lot of people, especially current users, do redeem coupons.

Let's deal with each of these problems.

Some people simply do not redeem coupons. Ironically, many low-income households will not take advantage of coupons. Conversely, some people are compulsive coupon redeemers. For reasons not completely understood by me, people with an Eastern European heritage are heavy coupon redeemers. In any case, more coupons go unredeemed than redeemed. In fact, about 97% of all those coupons that fall out of your newspaper on Sunday are never redeemed. So, marketers pay the cost of distributing all the coupons but get a sale in return for only about 3% of them.

This means that a huge percentage of the potential market for a given product can't or won't be reached by couponing. (I told you generating trial was difficult.)

Now for the other problem — that a lot of consumers, especially current users, do redeem coupons. If marketers get frustrated by paying to distribute coupons that never get redeemed, they can get equally frustrated by their inability to prevent current users from redeeming.

It certainly stands to reason that current users would redeem a coupon for their brand in disproportionate numbers. But you can't expect marketers to like it, because in effect, they're just subsidizing those users, reducing price and profit on a transaction from which they would normally get full price and profit from a loyal user.

Over the years, marketers have developed a rough formula for estimating the percentage of redemptions attributed to non-users of the product. This formula is 100 minus share times 90%. For example, if a product like Crest has a high share level (say 40%), then the equation should be (100 - 40) x .9 = 54%, i.e., 54% of the redemption is among non-users. As I said, this is rough, and it varies from brand to brand. Conversely, a product with a lower share level (for example, Ultra-Brite with 10%) could count on 81% of its redemption taking place among non-users — (100 - 10) x .9.

Now this does not mean high-share products shouldn't use coupons because they are largely rewarding current users. Nor does it mean couponing is always good for low-share products. Some of the non-users garnered by couponing the high-share product may switch and become loyal users, thereby building share even more. In the low-share case, the total redemption and conversion of non-users may be so low in absolute terms that the share gain wouldn't cover the cost of distributing the coupons. (For more discussion on trial, repeat and conversion, see Chapter Nineteen.)

Although the concepts and the math are simple, I've only scratched the surface of this promotion technique. Several other variables must be considered such as the face value of the coupon, the vehicle (newspaper, magazine, direct mail, on-package, in-package, etc.), frequency, season, day of the week, geography and, quite possibly, sunspot activity.

Furthermore, sampling and couponing are only two of dozens of consumer promotion techniques that are available. The list would also include temporary price reductions, tie-in offers (buy product X, get product Y for half price or get a coupon for product Y), on-pack premiums, mail-in premiums (buy Coppertone Lotion and get a free pair of sunglasses with proof of purchase), multiple purchase (buy two, get the third one free), sweepstakes, contests and on and on.

Determining the effectiveness of each of these is no less complicated than for couponing. Our clients have found there is no better way than continual experimentation, testing and research to find which promotions, over time, do the best job of meeting the strategic objectives of their brands.

You've probably noticed that I have been talking here only about "consumer promotions." The truth is, there is no such thing as a totally consumer promotion. Virtually none of these promotion techniques can be successful without retailer involvement of some kind.

If sampling and couponing are to work, the retailer must stock the product and redeem the coupons. For this, manufacturers pay slotting allowances and coupon handling charges. Retailers now typically collect $.08 from the manufacturer for every coupon redeemed, and studies have shown this barely covers the retailers' costs.

On top of this, manufacturers want retailers to stock special packs, beef up their inventories, build or use special temporary displays of product, run special prices and feature their promoted products in the stores' advertising. For this "performance," the manufacturers pay dearly in the form of "trade allowances."

In the past decade, with the rise of retailer power and the maturing of so many consumer market segments and product life cycles so that they now have relatively slow growth rates, the battle for market share among competing manufacturers has become fierce. Reams have been written about the use and misuse of promotion, not only in the war for share growth, but for short-term financial strategies, e.g., filling the pipeline to meet end-of-quarter or end-of-year sales goals. Over-use of promotions erodes category profitability and can have a harmful effect on brand image as well. It seems to many manufacturers that the more they spend on promotion, the more they have to spend on promotion, because nobody can afford to be the first to back down. This takes money away from image-building advertising which is already more expensive and less effective anyway for the reasons described in Chapter Five. It looks like a "no win" situation.

At HMG, we don't claim to know exactly how this problem will eventually be resolved, but we do believe it will happen. When the revolution comes, and we look back on it, I think we'll see that the "winners" of this conflict had several things in common. These will include, of course, continuing to offer good products at fair prices to meet the needs of consumers. But, in addition, these winners will have learned how, <u>through the aggressive and intelligent use of information</u>, to be the best at:

- being innovative in consumer promotion techniques.

- partnering with retailers.

- mastering the art, fast becoming almost a science, of effectively using both temporary and permanent displays.

- pioneering the other disciplines of in-store marketing.

In the next three chapters, I'll be discussing these last two areas in more depth, and naturally, with a slant toward how HMG and its clients intend to participate in the revolution.

CHAPTER EIGHT

From Metal-Bending to Mind-Bending: The Rise of the Display Business

Since the dawn of time, people have been bartering one ounce of X for two bales of Y. The most successful of these primitive retailers tried to increase the value of his merchandise by presenting the goods in the most appetizing fashion. He sought the most attractive presentation at the lowest possible cost.

Things didn't change much until recently, with the appearance and development of self-service retailing. As long as the salesman is there to sing the virtues of his product or to stick it under the nose of the prospective purchaser, there is little need to spend time and money developing an attractive presentation device. However, once the salesmen and the clerks stopped interacting with the consumers at the point of sale, something had to be developed to attract the attention of the consumers. That something is what we call a display.

Displays are the Rodney Dangerfields of the marketing profession — they "don't get no respect." You can look through learned marketing journals and marketing trade magazines, and you can go to marketing conferences and never see or hear a word about the power of displays. Yet, I have seen the results of literally hundreds of test panels covering dozens of product categories and multiple combinations of prices and promotional efforts, and *I have never seen anything as consistently effective in moving merchandise as off-shelf display.* I'm willing to wager that if you gave any knowledgeable marketing executive a choice between end-aisle displays in 15,000 supermarkets and another marketing alternative comparable in cost, he'd take the displays.

Let me emphasize that what I say is not a revelation to anyone in the marketing business who has studied test results over the past thirty years.

It's astounding, however, that neither manufacturers nor retailers have done much with the information. Many manufacturers offer display allowances and retailers accept these monies, but neither manufacturer nor retailer has really thought about the worth of a display in dollars-and-cents terms.

Few marketing executives can tell you how much incremental gross profit is generated by a ten-case, off-shelf display of their product. Yet, if they knew that such a display increased sales 300% (a number well within the realm of possibility in most categories) and that this increase translated into $40 of incremental gross profit, they could easily offer the retailer $20 for the display ($2 per case) and smile all the way to the bank.

This scenario is realistic for an overwhelming majority of products sold in mass retail outlets (supermarkets, drugstores and discounters). (See the Appendix to this chapter for the results of one definitive study.) Despite the diminished risk associated with it compared to other marketing options, most marketing executives spend little time considering it or plotting how to introduce it in 15,000 stores.

Until quite recently, retailers, too, have had no idea of the value of their display space. Sure, they realized products moved in great quantities off end aisles, and they realized manufacturers must be making something off this volume, but no one figured out the true worth. Retailers never realized that a company paying them $1 per case for a display might still be making an additional $4 per case profit. If retailers want to establish how valuable their display space is, they should conduct an auction for X weeks of display space by category. They would be astounded to find how much companies would bid for this prime space.

The power of the display is further underscored by the fact that a high percentage of shopping decisions are made on impulse after the consumer enters the store. Industry research concludes that 60% to 80% of shopping decisions are made in the store at the point of sale.

The importance of displays is another obvious factor in the

55

increased power of the retailer. The retailer can have a more immediate impact on sales by simply stacking merchandise in an aisle than Mr. Marketer can have with fancy advertising and couponing.

Manufacturers have piles of evidence proving the power of display, and their desire to obtain better displays created the industry which has been so good to me. But, with a few exceptions (like Sara Lee's L'eggs hosiery brand), off-shelf display has never been an important part of the marketing plan in most companies.

Indeed, it's been an afterthought industry. It was neither an art nor a science until companies like Howard Marlboro made it one.

The display business was really more — more of a hustle.

The Hustle

When I started in this business, display purchase was usually controlled by someone in the basement or the mailroom or in office supplies purchasing — rarely by the marketing department.

A few episodes from my early career as a display hustler will help you understand what a crazy business it was.

When I started the business, I targeted several industries. The liquor industry was top of the list. Distilleries were forbidden by law to use many of the marketing tools legally employed by other manufacturers. As a result, they spent lots on displays. We thought most of the displays weren't very imaginative, and we were brimming with ideas.

Unfortunately, we could not get our foot in the door. At that time, most of the big liquor houses were closed to new suppliers for reasons that weren't, shall we say, "wholesome." We needed a gimmick and we needed it bad. An article in a society column gave me an idea.

The article concerned one of the barons of the liquor industry, Sidney Rosensteil. It described a "Great Gatsby" party that Rosensteil had thrown at his estate on Long Island. Anyone who was anybody in New York society attended the party. The article went into minute detail regarding the lavish entertainment, the gourmet food and the elegant decorations. It was the party of the year. I wish I had been there, but I wasn't.

Nevertheless, the day after the party, I appeared at the desk of the secretary for the display buyer in Rosensteil's company. I had heard this buyer was mortally terrified of Mr. Rosensteil, his boss's boss. "Could I see Mr. X, the buyer?" I asked her.

"Do you have an appointment?"

"No," I answered truthfully, "but at the party last evening, Mr. Rosensteil suggested I contact Mr. X."

The secretary immediately changed her attitude and asked my name. "Just a moment," she said as she walked into Mr. X's office.

A moment later, Mr. X emerged wearing his suit jacket. "Mr. Wahl," he said, extending his hand, "won't you please come in?"

Mr. X immediately sought to understand my "relationship" with Mr. Rosensteil. I explained that I'd been fortunate enough to attend his party, and that Mr. Rosensteil had suggested I see him about some of my ideas. With one phone call, Mr. X could have blown my cover, ending my selling career with that company forever. But I had reasoned that no employee would risk Rosensteil's wrath by checking our "relationship." Mr. X didn't. Instead, he asked about my ideas.

As it turned out, Mr. X wasn't interested in my ideas, but he was very interested in pleasing "Mr. Rosensteil's friend." He gave me a nice order for a specific display that they had used in the past.

I returned in two weeks with my bid. Everyone in the office made a point of greeting me as I waited (briefly) in the anteroom. They all wanted to befriend Mr. Rosensteil's "friend." After some small talk with Mr. X, I submitted my bid for the display — "$3.90."

Mr. X looked at me as if I were crazy. "$4.80," he said.

"No, $3.90."

"$4.80," he repeated.

Suddenly, I got the idea. Mr. X helped me along. "The job is yours for $4.80. Don't break the price. We expect a lot from our suppliers."

That order was the start of a long, productive relationship with the company. I befriended Mr. X, and he never asked anything of me except that I not break prices, and that I put in a good word for him with my friend, Mr. Rosensteil.

Later on, Mr. X called on me more than once when he got into trouble. One memorable episode involved 500 Brazilian parrots.

Mr. Rosensteil was a creative guy. He knew that liquor laws prohibited almost all sorts of advertising but didn't exclude talking parrots. So Rosensteil bought 500 parrots and began to teach them advertising slogans before giving them to major liquor retailers. One of Rosensteil's major brands was Old Quaker, so the parrots were taught to say: "Polly wants Old Quaker." (I'm not making this up!)

Unfortunately for Mr. X, who was supervising the project, the parrots also picked up the filthiest, sexually-oriented, curse words. The parrots were caged close to the shipping department, and the men in the department hated the birds because they made noise and smelled awful. The employees, not the most genteel group in the world, vented their spleens on the hapless parrots by cursing them. The parrots reciprocated by repeating the curses. Of course, this delighted the men in shipping, but it caused Mr. X nightmares because Rosensteil wanted to get the birds out "selling."

"You're a creative guy, Mike," pleaded Mr. X. "How can I get out of this mess?" I had several suggestions, none of which would have passed muster with the Humane Society. Mr. X shook his head, convinced he would be eliminated when Rosensteil found out about his foul-mouthed fowls. The story has a bittersweet ending. The birds contracted a legitimate disease and starting dying in droves. With only a few left, Rosensteil decided to scrap the idea and gave away the few remaining birds.

Things as absurd as this were always happening in the display arena. It drove everybody crazy even though it was great fun and, in most instances, excellent for the client's business. By the way, I never did meet Mr. Rosensteil. He passed away a few years ago, with my "cover" still intact.

Answering the Wrong Question

As time went by, we realized that clients' businesses would be even healthier if we could enhance the ordinary, day-to-day, non-promotional presentation of the product.

Clients would come in and ask for a cheap display for a temporary promotion. We would give it to them instead of asking, "How should this product be presented day in, day out?" We realized we were committing one of the cardinal sins of business. We were answering the wrong question.

We began insisting that clients ask the larger question. Once we began answering the right question, our clients respected us even more. They saw us as more than "metal benders." They saw us as valuable members of their marketing team. Our business took off because our clients' businesses took off.

Of course, it didn't happen overnight. It took years of hard work and solid results to earn our clients' respect. Sometimes we earned it in a strange way.

You remember the Pillsbury refrigerated dough organizer I discussed earlier? That was a turning point in our relationship with Pillsbury. The sales manager of refrigerated dough was Jim Carroll, an ex-Marine who kept a gold combat boot on his desk to show that he "kicked ass" when necessary. Jim was a gruff-voiced, heart-of-gold type who enjoyed the give and take of price negotiations. Shortly after the organizer was successfully tested, Pillsbury put the first order out to bid — a contract worth several million dollars. To Jim Carroll's chagrin (and mine, too, as it turned out), our bid to build units we had designed came in 10% higher than the competition's bid. Jim Carroll called and said, "Mike, get your ass to Minneapolis tomorrow!" I got on a plane and went.

Jim, in his usual fashion, began screaming at me about our pricing.

I replied, "Tell me how much this idea's worth." He looked at me with a blank stare, so I continued. "I'll reduce my price, not by 10% but by 40%, if you give me 10% of the extra profit you make over a two-year period on the system we develop."

Jim, in typical Marine fashion said, "It's a deal!"

I walked out saying to myself, "Oh my God, I could lose a fortune."

But I had enough faith from the test results of the organizer to believe I had done the right thing. Ten percent of the incremental profit we expected to generate over a two-year period would come to over $1 million. This would have given me about 500% more than I was asking on my pricing.

Several months later, a different Jim Carroll called me and said, "Mike, when would it be convenient for you to come to Minneapolis, or would you like me to come to New York?" I went to Minneapolis, and Jim treated me to a wonderful lunch. He told me that my pricing was fine, but asked if I would forego the 10% of incremental profits we had agreed upon. Needless to say, I forgave the 10% and went back to our original pricing. Pillsbury is still a client twenty years later!

Despite our success as a company, our field still doesn't command the respect of other disciplines involved in marketing, especially that accorded to the highly visible advertising agencies and their "product." But a delicious irony is playing itself out. As advertising becomes less and less effective, everyone is getting more and more conscious of the importance and power of in-store effort. As one wag put it, "The war is in the store." Well, it is, and we are one of the few companies which has spent all of its energies figuring out how to impact the consumer at the point of sale.

One good example of impact is how our experience helped us pioneer the development of the first major, consumer-interactive, shelf-edge computer.

Noxell's Clarion Line

We had been working with Noxell for years, developing a relationship of trust and mutual benefit.

They came to us with a challenge more and more marketers will soon face. Noxell was developing a line of cosmetics with special performance characteristics. Choosing the correct combination of products required information about the individual purchaser. In days gone by, this product would have been sold in department stores where a sales clerk could elicit the information from the customer and recommend an appropriate purchase based on her knowledge of the line.

But Noxell wanted to reach the mass market where there are no clerks to help the consumer. Their challenge to us: design an interactive, point-of-sale computer to replace the clerks, allowing the consumer to choose the right products based on the computer's recommendation from information the customer provides.

When I heard this, I realized how much the world had changed. When we started bending metal, we were an afterthought to corporate management. Now we were approached by the top executives of the most successful mass market cosmetics company in America to help them solve a fundamental problem relating to the changes in the retail environment.

Meeting the Noxell challenge required technical skill we lacked. We formed a new company, MarkitStar, that combined our knowledge of the consumer and retail marketplace with the requisite technological skills. Within a few months, we had developed and tested a prototype, made working models and placed them in a market situation.

The six-month results were incredible. Noxell decided to expand their Clarion line with our computer as an integral part of the marketing plan.

Clarion was the most successful cosmetics introduction in the 1980's thanks in no small measure to the MarkitStar-designed, shelf-edge computers which were placed (and remain) in over 30,000 retail outlets.

We believe the Clarion computer signals a new age in retailing, an age characterized by information-hungry consumers seeking personalized answers to their needs in a retail environment devoid of adequate human sales assistance. We believe companies like HMG and MarkitStar, which combine a knowledge of the point of sale with computer skills, can become as important to the overall marketing equation in the 1990's as advertising agencies and promotion consulting firms were in the 1960's.

Appendix to Chapter Eight

For years, we "knew" in-store effort was the most powerful weapon in grocery marketing. Now someone has finally proved it.

Throughout 1988, in a study called "Topical Marketing Reports," Information Resources, Inc. used its supermarket scanning capability to measure the relative impact of price-off, display, ad features, and combinations thereof, across 164 categories in 2,400 stores in 66 geographically-dispersed markets in the United States.

The results:

- Every category showed increases from display.

- A single week of display gets as much extra volume as eight weeks of unadvertised, on-shelf price discounting alone.

- On the average, displays were more effective than retail best food day ad features.

(What would you expect when most decisions are made in the store on impulse?)

The following table shows the results for 31 of the 164 categories included in the study. The table can be read as follows: suppose in the normal week, with no effort of any kind, paper towel movement equaled 100 units. Reducing the price by 15%, with no other effort, increased unit movement to 158 per week, a 58% increase. Featuring paper towels in the weekly newspaper ad at 15% off, but leaving towels on-shelf rather than on-display, caused unit movement of 500. Moving the product off shelf onto a display with the 15% price reduction increased movement to 741 units per week. Combining all the promotion options (15% price reduction, ad feature and off-shelf display) increased weekly unit movement to 1,096, or almost 11 times more than normal weekly movement with no promotional effort.

EFFECT OF VARIOUS PROMOTIONAL OPTIONS
(Selected Categories)
(Normal Week Indexed at 100)

	15% Price Reduction Only	Price Reduction With Ad Feature Only	Price Reduction With Display	Price Reduction With Both
Bakery Department				
Department Average	130	279	382	550
Pies & Cakes	152	299	471	621
Bakery Snacks	142	334	451	698
English Muffins	126	300	360	586
French Bread & Rolls	127	271	316	497
Dairy Department				
Department Average	131	256	361	585
Yogurt	127	268	521	724
Pickles & Relish	128	212	442	380*
Cheese	135	253	333	487
Sour Cream	123	221	266	568
Deli Department				
Department Average	132	269	454	749
Frankfurters	135	286	540	723
Sausage	140	290	530	1075
Breakfast Meats	132	319	510	803
Deli Lunch Meats	127	209	354	555
Edible Groceries Department				
Department Average	136	278	385	628
Seafood (Shelf-Stable)	145	469	635	1170
Vegetables (Shelf-Stable)	139	350	600	992
Cocktail Mixes	133	188	255	317
Drink Mixes	133	240	243	406

	15% Price Reduction Only	Price Reduction With Ad Feature Only	Price Reduction With Display	Price Reduction With Both
Frozen Foods Department				
Department Average	132	277	457	745
Frozen Seafood	137	300	573	887
Frozen Juices	140	342	565	836
Ice Cream	129	280	373	636
Frozen Fruit	128	231	289	524
Health & Beauty Aids Department				
Department Average	131	233	256	415
Oral Hygiene	136	219	873	1244**
Misc. Health Tablets	144	219	601	443**
Cough Drops	132	203	210	282
Cough Syrup	136	197	187	232
Non-Edible Groceries				
Department Average	138	289	429	831
Toilet Tissue	162	541	809	1108
Paper Towels	158	500	741	1096
Sanitary Protection	125	194	238	315
Pest Control	143	233	202	289
General Merchandise Department				
Department Average	124	201	257	445
Coffee Filters	124	239	297	528
Foil Pans	129	218	285	641
Hosiery	122	186	239	405
Total of 164 Categories	**135**	**273**	**379**	**645**

SOURCE: Information Resources, Inc., Chicago, as published in *P-O-P TIMES*, January/February, 1990 and July/August, 1991
* Small Base
** Very Small Base

Part II

CHAPTER NINE
The In-Store Consultant

When HMG was a struggling young company, someone asked me what we did. I went into a long-winded explanation, hoping that the gentleman who asked would find something in my laundry list of skills that he would want to buy.

After a while, he concluded, "Now I understand. You're a consultant."

I started to object, but then I shrugged and agreed with him. "You're right, I'm sort of an in-store consultant."

Initially, I was somewhat offended to be called a consultant, but as the years have gone by, I've become rather enamored of the idea. In the first place, there's nothing wrong with a profession that accumulates usable, accurate knowledge, then expands upon that base of knowledge and conveys the knowledge to others in a way that helps them make money.

More importantly, there's certainly nothing wrong with, and a lot of things right about, being an "in-store consultant," because no one else in America is doing it the way HMG does. No one else has taken the unified, systematic, integrated approach to the point of sale that we have.

Astonishing as it may seem, the part of the marketing experience where 60% to 80% of purchase decisions are made, and the location where 100% of cash changes hands (i.e., inside the store) has been almost totally ignored by major marketing services companies. Sure, many companies focus on one segment or another, but no one studies the whole environment like HMG.

When I look back at our growth and our acquisition by Saatchi & Saatchi, I recognize that both happened because we were focusing on the most vital segment of the marketing process, the in-store experience. I'm not claiming that we knew everything then or know everything now about the in-store experience. What I am saying is that we were successful because the industry realized we were focusing on a critical issue when very few of our competitors seemed to care one iota about the unglamorous aisles of America's stores.

How We Got This Way

Many people wonder how we got as big as we are without being squashed by huge competitors who use their size as a competitive advantage. Many people can't understand how ad agencies ever let a business like ours slip out of their grasp or, more accurately, grow to maturity outside their tent.

I always thought that an advertising agency seemed a natural place for a business like HMG to grow and flourish. We function as part of the marketing process — an important part, but a part nonetheless. It seemed natural that ad agencies with an abundance of creative resources, the responsibility for The Big Picture and access to corporate pocketbooks, would create and build a business resembling HMG.

Why didn't it happen? Why did we wind up being acquired by a large agency? The second question is easier to answer than the first. We were acquired because Saatchi & Saatchi realized that HMG provided a profitable service that they did not offer. I realized they could help us grow, and they wanted the privilege of offering us to their clients.

The more difficult question is why didn't the larger agencies develop an "in-store consultant" like us internally? The answer is "marketing myopia." Like the Pennsylvania Railroad, which thought it was in the railroad business instead of the transportation business and missed the growth of trucking, ad agencies focused on the advertising business and forgot they were in the selling business.

Well into the 1980's, agencies focused their energies on the art of making commercials. They rewarded that function almost exclusively, and they failed to train management to look at the larger picture for their clients.

As a result, they lost control of their clients. Marketing executives in large corporations, who should have been leaning on an experienced agency executive to help provide them with an integrated presence in the marketplace, found themselves instead talking to dozens of specialists, like HMG, who'd developed an expertise greatly valued in the marketplace and ignored by the agencies.

In a way, the agencies were victims of their own success and a technological quirk known as television. For the thirty-year period between 1950 and 1980, the power and popularity of TV and TV advertising grew so fast that it was impossible not to make money. For writing, producing and buying commercials to be aired on network TV, the agency was paid 15% of the air time value in perpetuity. Now I know agencies did a lot more than get fat off network TV, but that was the backbone of the business, and boy, was it profitable!

No wonder agency execs took their eye off the ball. Why worry about all these other disciplines when TV was so powerful and profitable? The rest, as they say, is history. While agencies abdicated their natural role, whole industries were created to fill the vacuum.

For example, large promotion development companies sprang from practically nothing to the point where some, although unknown to the general public, are more profitable than glittery New York agencies. The marketing consulting profession grew from virtually nothing in 1986 to the point where it has swallowed the town of Westport, Connecticut, with every street corner sporting its own consulting boutique.

In what must seem like the ultimate irony, media buying services began popping up, enabling clients to contract for this service at a low rate and then go to the agencies and buy creative services "by the pound."

The ultimate nightmare of the advertising industry has now become reality. A client can "unbundle" and buy separate, high quality services at low prices, ending up with higher quality overall services at lower overall costs.

Every large, well-run agency will admit that this "unbundling" threatens the profitability of their industry. Many are taking steps to combat it. Our parent company, Saatchi & Saatchi, addressed the problem by acquiring niche companies, like HMG, to complement its advertising agencies like Compton, DFS, Ted Bates and Campbell-Mithun.

Other agencies have taken a different approach. For example, Lintas is retraining its top executives to re-establish control of the entire marketing process with their clients. They are forcing these executives to sit through classroom study on arcane subjects like Yellow Pages advertising and in-store advertising so that they can credibly represent to their clients that they can create a comprehensive, multi-faceted plan uniquely suited to the clients' needs.

What We Do

I understand what Lintas is trying to do. It should have been done twenty years ago by every large agency. I doubt very seriously that late blooming efforts like this can compensate for HMG's thirty years of focus on the store aisle and everything that happens there. It's too much to ask one person, no matter how intelligent and well-meaning, to master all the details of every aspect of the marketing process. Even one discipline, like "in-store consulting," covers a remarkable range of issues.

For example, at HMG, we in-store consultants have to understand everything there is to know about the following:

- Strategic marketing planning
- Package design
- Shipping container design
- Off-shelf displays
- On-shelf merchandising and display
- Gondola design (stocking rates, etc.)
- Pallet displays
- In-store advertising
- In-store promotion
- Direct product profit models
- In-store labor handling issues

- Store layout and design
- Customer traffic patterns
- Interactive, electronic point of sale
- In-store-related marketing research techniques
- The interrelationships of all the above

Any one of these can be (and has been) the subject of extensive study by individual suppliers, manufacturers, retailers, consultants, academicians and industry groups. At HMG, we make it our business to stay on top of the latest acquired data and to conduct our own studies because in-store is our business, our only business, and it's where 60% to 80% of all buying decisions are made. We want to know: What are the facts? What do people think the facts are? How are people reacting to these facts? What don't we know? Here are a couple of examples:

Direct Product Profit

One of the most fascinating areas of recent development is the use of *direct product profit* models by retailers. These computer-driven models attempt to answer what seems to be a simple question for retailers. How much money are they making on a specific product?

I say "seems to be a simple question" because retailers used to answer the question by subtracting their cost for a can of X from their selling price, and voilà, there was their profit. For years, many retailers understood that "the cost was not the cost" of a can of X. They realized that different products cost more to handle than others. Then, in the early 1970's, consultants and academicians developed a new way of thinking about profitability and began selling this new way of thinking to retailers.

This new thinking is known as "direct product profit," or DPP. Even this sophisticated concept is easy to explain. Start with what you paid for the product, increase the cost by all the handling and warehousing you can readily assign to that product, decrease it by any special deals, payment terms, etc., and you arrive at a real, adjusted cost. Now, subtract this cost from the selling price to get a real "direct product profit."

Unfortunately, during the early days of DPP exploration, many manufacturers took a highly mechanistic, simplified view of the output from the formulas and made lots of silly, wrong-headed recommendations about their products and categories. The retailers, who were behind the power curve on understanding and utilizing DPP in the first place, immediately saw through a lot of these recommendations and turned their skepticism, not on the bad recommendations, but on DPP as a tool.

As a result, many retailers lost years of time and millions in profit dragging their feet on DPP utilization. Several things eventually changed retailer attitudes. First was the mountain of data accumulating in storerooms from the new generation of electronic cash registers and scanners. Second was the hiring by retailers of young, computer-literate accountants who were able to develop models using chain- and store-specific data that were inherently more credible than manufacturer data. Third was the growing realization that something had to be done about lousy financial results from the supermarket industry.

Overriding all of these factors was the retailers' realization that DPP and its various aspects had something to do with their two biggest assets — their shelf space and their consumers. As retailers realized that DPP could get them a higher return per foot of space and satisfy more customers, interest in the system increased dramatically.

A brief digression will help explain how this works. Suppose Category A has five brands with fifteen different sizes and flavors on the shelf, all taking up the same space, selling at the same price, generating the same profit and moving off the shelf at the same speed. The stockboy can easily keep pace with demand and restock the shelf on a regular basis. Out-of-stocks are at a minimum; consumers are happy. Just for the record, this situation exists nowhere in the Western World.

Now, let's go to the real world. Manufacturer A introduces a new item with a different size package and a higher price. Consumers love it. They start snapping it up. Out-of-stocks occur. Customers are unhappy. Sales are lost. Indicated action — reset the shelf. Give more space to the products that customers want.

Once retailers understood that DPP and shelf space models could increase profit per foot and please more customers, we were off and running. Retailers even began paying attention to manufacturers' presentations again. Some manufacturers were able to produce truly remarkable computer-generated analyses that compared two different stocking models of a category to reveal how too much space for slow-moving products crowded out fast-moving products, reduced profitability and disappointed consumers.

My personal favorite was a presentation of a huge category with lots of different brands and sizes. Manufacturer A had been visiting the store five times a week to stock and restock their popular brands which were flying out of the store and were out of stock constantly. Manufacturer B was visiting the store twice a week, spreading their slow-moving brands across the shelves and not suffering any out-of-stocks because movement was disproportionately small compared to facings.

Incredibly, the retailer was mad at Manufacturer A for "bad service levels." Every time Manufacturer A asked for more space, they were told, "You can't keep the space we give you full." Finally, with the aid of computer simulation, our beleaguered Manufacturer A was able to show that more space for them would result in fewer out-of-stocks, more total category sales, fresher product for consumers and fewer disappointed consumers.

The turning point in the presentation occurred when one of the chain executives turned to his subordinates and said, "My God, those other guys are using our shelves as their warehouse."

The use of these computerized models is advancing rapidly now. Retailers all over America are constantly reshuffling categories to insure their keeping pace with manufacturers' new product offerings and the changing consumer purchase patterns.

The most sophisticated retailers now vary their product mix and space store by store so that they respond to the unique purchasing pattern of the neighborhood.

For example, if you know what different socio-economic groups patronize Store A, and you know product consumption patterns by group, you can model virtually every category in the store and arrive at an optimum mix within and among categories (e.g., the salad dressing category should get X% of the space, and it should be divided among the brands as follows).

But wait! Just as the computer jockeys and data base suppliers were about to capture control of America with this line of analysis, somebody realized that it's possible to have too much of a good thing. As one retailer said, "We are about to improve ourselves right out of business. If we follow this analysis to its logical conclusion, we'll sell nothing but soft drinks, potato chips and pantyhose."

What this experienced retailer was really saying was quite profound. Retailers need to make sure that they design stores for customers and not to please their accountants. They need to remember why customers come to supermarkets in the first place (one-stop shopping), and they need to remember concepts like brand loyalty.

Let me expand on this a little. A rigorous mathematical analysis might lead a retailer to conclude that he was making no money on fresh meat. ("All that space, all those union butchers, all that refrigeration equipment, all that cholesterol, all that blood — get it outta here.") Then ask yourself how many customers are regular patrons of a supermarket with no fresh meat.

Now that may seem an absurd example, but this kind of reasoning could apply to literally dozens of products within a store. And, if the supermarket retailer were to embrace that reasoning, he would undermine the basic reason for his industry's existence.

A related, somewhat more subtle, concept is consumer loyalty and intensity of preference. In some categories, a small group of consumers intensely prefer specific brand variants which take up room on the shelf. Even the most rigorous mathematical analysis today will not compensate for intensity of preference. Therefore, a recommendation that the highly-preferred, but slow-moving, Brand A be dropped tends to imply that its consumers will switch within the category to Brand B, when, in actuality, they will buy nothing from the category.

In fact, if this happens too many times in too many categories, these customers will search until they find a store that will satisfy their needs. As a result, major retailers are scurrying to find loyalty formulas to enhance the DPP formulas. The smart retailers already know that loyalty varies dramatically by category and brand, so that DPP formulas can be used rigorously in some places in the store but very carefully in others.

The issue boils down to one of retail strategy and objectives. What kind of store do I want customers to think I am? What kind of stocking model delivers on that promise? What are my risks and rewards? How do I measure success?

From a manufacturer's perspective, one must remember that each brand and category plays a slightly different role in this equation. Each category, brand and size responds slightly differently. "In-store consultants" know these things, and selling them keeps the electric bill paid.

In-Store Advertising

At HMG, we spend time and money to stay on top of DPP. Meanwhile, another explosion has occurred in-store where we live. It's called in-store advertising.

For years, the only in-store advertising vehicle was the little cardboard sign on the shopping cart. In the last five years, we've seen lots of new entrants. Signs over the aisles, signs on the shelf, neon signs in the aisles, in-store radio, in-store TV, TV's on shopping carts, electronic kiosks, proximity-activated radio, pre-programmed interactive, etc. Each of these new, in-store media affects shoppers differently by brand. Each has a cost structure. I could write several chapters on this topic alone. The point is, if you're an "in-store consultant," you keep up with these things.

CHAPTER TEN
The Rules of the Game for In-Store Marketing

In the old days, we basically looked at advertising, promotion, package design and sales as the disciplines to be mastered in order to claim packaged goods marketing expertise. Many other "lesser" elements of marketing, particularly those having to do with the in-store environment, were treated almost as afterthoughts, assigned as training for assistant product managers and often delegated to the purchasing department. Rarely did the president or chairman of the company get involved.

These elements are not new on the marketing scene. At HMG, we've made a very successful business of paying close attention to these elements (many of which are listed in Chapter Nine) because we have long known that, when taken together, and when planned and executed in concert with the traditional disciplines of marketing, they do form something entirely new that has only recently begun to be recognized as such.

What is it?

To borrow a line from Herman Melville, "Call it in-store marketing."

In 1991, I was asked to chair a seminar on in-store marketing called Merchandising Magic which was presented by the Babcock Graduate School of Management at Wake Forest University. If graduate business schools are recognizing this field, it's clearly time for the marketing community to do the same.

In Europe, Sara Lee Corporation has appointed a vice president of in-store marketing, and Cornelis Boonstra, who is chairman of the management board there, has made it his personal project to move the sales needle forward. This is happening more and more in various companies.

Maybe it began as a "hustle," like advertising, promotion and selling did, but now there is a discipline surrounding it, just as there is in other fields. Don't get me wrong, there is still a lot of creativity and innovation involved. An environment of free-spirited thinking is absolutely required. Discipline is applied simply to insure getting the most out of the process.

Over the years at HMG, we have developed a set of guidelines and principles that we think describes what is necessary for a successful in-store marketing program. We call it "The Rules of the Game." "Rules" provide a framework for the discipline required to get the most out of the effort of trying to do a good job. By its nature, in-store marketing involves the integration of many different elements that have to work together. Ideally, the elements complement each other so that the whole ends up being greater than the sum of its parts. When the result is a unified program that reinforces and builds on consumer recognition by looking pretty much the same from store to store (and also, ideally relates well to the advertising), the resulting synergies maximize the impact of the program and give you the most bang for your in-store marketing buck.

A good set of rules starts with definitions. What is "in-store marketing?"

Definition

> In-store marketing is a strategic process for satisfying the in-store wants and needs of the <u>consumer</u> and the in-store business requirements of the <u>retailer</u>.

Since most of our clients are manufacturers, this definition is, admittedly, written from a manufacturer's point of view. "Well, if that's true," you might ask, "where does it talk about satisfying the manufacturer's needs?" Good question. Obviously, you, the manufacturer, are not going to ignore your own objectives and limitations in some benighted crusade to give the consumer and the retailer everything they say they want. But these are your customers, they are why you are in business. Their wants and needs must be understood and addressed in order for your own to have any chance of success. (It should go without saying that the definition applies equally to retailers and advertisers, indeed all marketers, but there, I said it anyway.)

Okay, what about the rules? Let me list them first before commenting on each of them.

The Rules

1. Define and Accept the Vision.

2. Prioritize: You Can't Do Everything.

3. Understand and Address the Retail Reality.

4. Understand and Apply the Discipline of In-Store Marketing.

Rule #1: Define and Accept the Vision.

First and foremost, someone has to develop the vision for "what we are going to look like in the store." This should be treated as an important part of the marketing plan. In fact, In-Store Marketing should have its own heading in the strategy, objectives and tactical plan sections, because only then can the marketer be certain that there is a place to include all the elements which, in prior years' plans, were scattered throughout the document, sometimes omitted and rarely strategically integrated in execution. The vision and plan should be based upon research and testing and should call for assessment and revision as experience is gained in the marketplace.

Part of the vision statement would include a priority list of negotiable elements. Maybe there are well-founded reasons why every element of the vision cannot be implemented in its ideal form. For example, maybe it turns out to be prohibitively expensive for every flat surface of our cosmetics display to be polished to a mirror finish. In that case, maybe we have to compromise — "total mirrors" becomes a negotiable element. In no way, however, will we give up on the requirement that at least one mirror somehow be a prominent feature of the display.

Next, you have to get top management approval. Usually, this is part of the marketing plan approval process, but it is important that explicit top management approval of the in-store marketing plan be obtained. Top management certainly wants to approve the advertising, doesn't it? Not only is good advertising important in moving the sales needle, it can shape the image of your whole company. (It can also be embarrassing if the board of directors doesn't like it, it receives bad press for tastelessness or not being "politically correct," or any number of other reasons.) Top management should be even more interested in the in-store marketing plan because, especially with the decline of advertising impact discussed previously, the store is now where the company and its products are primarily represented to the consumer, as well as to the other constituents with whom top management must be concerned.

In addition, unlike advertising which is pretty tightly controlled in its execution by the marketing people and the advertising agency, in-store marketing consists of a large number of elements that must be executed by diverse groups of people inside and outside the company, and there are many opportunities for compromise and the advancement of conflicting, off-strategy agendas. Top management approval gives the in-store marketing plan and all its elements a stamp of authority about which most people will think twice before trifling.

Once it's approved, the next step is to get everyone on board with the plan. This means primarily the salesforce, but it can also include other departments of the company such as manufacturing, distribution and customer service. Even if everyone accepts the plan and wants to "do it right," the complexity of it requires that you educate everyone on the policies, philosophies and executional aspects of the plan. If special and repeated training is required, do it. If speeches and messages from the company president are required, get them.

Finally, you must control and monitor the execution of the plan. Feedback and reports from the salesforce, field trips, interviews with the trade, even consumer research are required to know how well the program is working. You may not get it right the first time. If not, don't be afraid to make changes. The plan should state specifically how you intend to carry out the control, monitoring and reassessment processes.

In summary:

- Include "The Vision" in the marketing plan as a specific subject.

- Develop priority lists of negotiable elements.

- Gain top management approval.

- Educate the salesforce and others on policy and philosophy.

- Control and monitor at salesforce/trade level.

- Assess and revise after test and experience.

The main point here is that the commitment to in-store marketing has to run throughout the organization. It must be recognized as an essential element in the marketing mix. Everyone must share the vision.

To insure a continuation of excellence in in-store marketing planning and execution, I recommend appointing an "in-store marketing manager" to be the champion of the process, the caretaker of the discipline, the focal point for execution of the elements and the mentor of those in the organization who would learn more about this important field. Obviously, this person should be senior enough in the organization to have some clout. If the position itself is not at the vice presidential or equivalent level (as is the case with Sara Lee in Europe), it should certainly report to that level.

Rule #2: Prioritize — You Can't Do Everything.

The strategic commitment referred to in Rule #1 requires tough decisions on where to devote time, effort and funds. There is a long list of elements in the in-store marketing plan and an even longer list of great executional ideas that the marketing people and your agencies, ideally with input from retailers, will come up with. Someone has to decide which ones are truly on strategy and are most likely to drive the sales of your brand or category; which ones, when put together in a "package," will do the best job of taking the desired brand image and profit story into the store for the benefit of the consumer and the retailer.

Even if you could do everything eventually, you couldn't do it all at once. Therefore, you must prioritize on a timeline, and quite possibly, geographically and customer-by-customer. For example, introducing a new package nationally cannot be done overnight. A specific plan must be written on what to do with the old packaging. This might mean transshipping it to designated "flush-out" markets which will be the last ones to get the new packaging. This can take months.

New display installation requires major in-store activity for which retailers must plan far in advance. Some retailers have a policy of doing this only once a year at most. So even if all your customers accept your plan immediately (which they won't), you must work with them on the timetable that best suits them, unless you can provide appropriate incentives to get them to change their schedules.

Your advertising and promotion plans will have to take into account these timing and priority issues, both in terms of creative content and scheduling.

Prioritize. Decide what you <u>must</u> do (essential for the strategy to work) and what you <u>can</u> do (realistically, given the resources of your company and those of the retailers, your agencies and suppliers), and either save the rest for later or cross it off your list.

Rule #3: Understand and Address the <u>Retail Reality</u>.

Remember what's going on out there. You, the consumer and the trade all have different agendas. You are thinking about your <u>brand</u>, the consumer is thinking about <u>convenience and saving time</u>, and the trade is thinking about all of this from a <u>category</u> perspective.

Remember some of the trends we have already talked about. Retail profit margins are small, and self-service is increasing. Stores are getting bigger. The number of items available is becoming staggeringly large. Therefore, <u>shoppability</u> is becoming an increasing problem for the consumer, hence, the importance of focusing on this element in any in-store merchandising plan.

Consumers are making more and more of their purchase decisions right there in the store — about 70% today on average for all products, both for food and non-food. Brand loyalty is decreasing, reinforcing the shift in retail decision-making power toward the retailer and away from the manufacturer.

The manufacturer wants a higher share of the category in which he is involved, higher sales of his brands and more space in the store. The retailer, on the other hand, is concerned with his productivity in terms of his share of the retail market in his trading area, sales of whole categories and profit per square foot as measured by such techniques as DPP.

Central to the art of negotiating is understanding what the other party really wants and needs, and trying to find a way to give it to him while seeing that your own needs are also met. So should it be with your in-store marketing plan.

Rule #4: Understand and Apply the Discipline of In-Store Marketing.

I don't want to turn this into a textbook on in-store marketing because I need to keep the options open for my next book, but you will understand why I mention this after I give you a brief summary of some key issues and considerations involved in what makes in-store marketing a discipline.

From a retailer's point of view, here are the in-store marketing issues. How does your in-store marketing plan measure up on addressing these factors?

- Space efficiency potential — facings per horizontal and vertical foot of selling space

- Product presentation potential — eye appeal, effective point-of-sale communication, e.g., size, color, flavor and price

- Potential labor savings — easy to stack and price-mark; store labor vs. manufacturer or "rack jobber," etc.

- Pack-out potential — units or packages of product per square or cubic foot of selling space

- Velocity potential — how fast the product moves

All of the above add up to an improvement, or "dis-improvement," in retailer profitability.

Against the background of these issues, the retailer must attempt to optimize his in-store opportunity. His criterion is profitability, but his customer, the shopper, has a different criterion — shoppability. The retailer and the manufacturer are engaged in a balancing act with merchandising considerations such as:

- Assortment
- Facings
- Organization of product (sometimes called a planogram)
- Location
- Fixture design
- Store layout
- Advertising
- Package design
- Inventory
- Price

Each of these must be viewed in light of the in-store marketing issues above in order to achieve the desired balance of shoppability and retailer profitability.

Discipline can and must be applied to each of these merchandising considerations. Fortunately, although it can be carried to extremes, all of these considerations can be subjected to research and testing, either by themselves or in combination with one another. Consumer intercept studies, in-store consumer tracking, product and packaging use studies, etc., are popular consumer research techniques that can provide important quantitative data for decision-making. Other observational and attitudinal research techniques, which can be qualitative or quantitative, include focus groups, in-store video observation, store audits, photo audits and interviews with retail managers, buyers and headquarters executives. Simulations can be run where consumers are asked to "shop in mock stores" to gauge their reactions to planograms, package designs, pricing or any number of other variables. Useful information can also be obtained from consumer-interactive computers that are programmed to keep track of the interaction with the consumer such as personal information, shade, size or flavor selection, etc. Finally, full-fledged test marketing in small towns or limited geographic areas can still be done, although its cost has become almost prohibitive.

Well, those are the "rules." There are no formulas or recipes here. Obviously, we haven't programmed a computer with all these issues, considerations and guidelines to manipulate a huge data base that allows us to plug in your particular problem and come up with the "answer" to in-store marketing for brand X. I hope we never do.

When we started years ago, none of us could have envisioned the degree of sophistication that has developed around this business. What started as a hustle and evolved into an art has not yet, I am relieved to say, become completely a science. At HMG, we're not about to let discipline stifle creativity. On the other hand, when we come up with a great creative idea, you can be equally sure we will apply the appropriate discipline to let us know just how great it really is... or isn't... before we let a client bet the future of his company on it.

PART III
Europe and The Implications of
Global Marketing

CHAPTER ELEVEN

1992

I used to go to Europe on vacation to relax. Now I go on business to make money.

The reason is simple. From now until the end of the 20th Century, more change will occur in commercial relations in Western Europe than at any time since the opening of the new world transformed the economies of the great European empires. It is quite conceivable that the year 1992 (when a true European Common Market is scheduled to come into being) will someday have the same meaning to a European that 1776 does to an American.

When you add the legal changes scheduled to culminate in 1992 to the on-going revolution in communications sweeping across Europe, you have change of epic proportions. Change means opportunity. That's why we have opened offices in several major cities in Europe. We want to bring our knowledge of in-store merchandising to Europe.

This whole situation is more than a little ironic in several respects.

For the past ten years, one of the most unappreciated trends in American business has been the steady growth in the ownership of American grocery retailers by European companies. This was driven home to me recently by a friend who called me, quite startled about a Japanese supermarket named Yaohan, which had just opened in Edgewater, New Jersey, south of the George Washington Bridge on the Hudson River across from Manhattan.

According to my friend, this was a "test market" for the Japanese who were going to "buy up" all the supermarkets in America. I knew about Yaohan, and I'd been in the store, so I could assure my friend that this was a very special store catering primarily to the large population of relocated Japanese businessmen and their families who live in the Edgewater area.

"This isn't a test of anything that can be expanded broadly in the U.S.," I assured my friend. "It's a Japanese store for a clientele that is 90% Japanese. The products and packaging are even printed in Japanese." Then I really laid it on my friend. "If you're so concerned about foreigners buying American grocery stores, why didn't you call when Tenglemann's bought control of A&P?"

"What?" my friend said. "The Germans own A&P?"

"Only a little over 50%," I said trying to comfort her.

"Well, that's it. From now on, I'm shopping at Food Emporium [a real nice, up-scale chain in metro New York]."

I could barely keep from laughing out loud. "Tenglemann's controls them too."

I went on to make several points to my friend. A&P is a much better run operation today than they were ten years ago before Tenglemann's bought in, so, if anything, A&P customers were a net winner because of "foreign" ownership.

Next, I pointed out that many American grocery retailers are totally owned or controlled by Europeans. For example, Food Lion, an extremely successful North Carolina-based chain, is controlled by Delhaize, a Belgian company. Shaw's, in New England, is owned by Sainsbury's of England. Other joint ventures between U.S. and foreign retailers are almost too numerous to mention.

The third thing I pointed out to my friend was why these retailers came to America — an opportunity to grow. Until quite recently, European retailers have been locked into a low-growth or no-growth situation. Population in many European countries is not growing at all — in some, declining. In many countries, rigorous laws prohibit or discourage new sites. Moreover, a European grocery retailer seldom builds outside his home country, so a Dutch firm is locked into The Netherlands where the population is less than metro New York, and a French firm feels bound by the borders of France with a population much smaller than that of the states which once formed the

Southern Confederacy.

By the time I got through explaining their plight, my friend was practically feeling sorry for the European retailers. I didn't even take the time or have the heart to point out that the same problems which have caused the European retailers to invest in the United States have caused many European manufacturers to invest here as well. Major U.S. brands, such as Lean Cuisine, Carnation, even the Pillsbury Dough Boy and many, many others are now owned by "foreign" companies headquartered in Western Europe.

If anything, the problems of the European manufacturer were even more discouraging than those facing the European retailer. French law was set up to protect French companies and, by implication, to discriminate against non-French companies. The same can be said for Italian law, German law, etc.

As if this weren't enough, an enterprising company wishing to "export" from Italy to Belgium or from Spain to Denmark (approximately the distance from Dallas to Chicago) would be caught in a web of bureaucratic red tape.

Someone once calculated that a truck of merchandise in transit from one end of Western Europe to another could be stopped for customs up to five times, forced to pay numerous taxes, required to wait for time-consuming inspections, made to transfer loads to various domestic carriers and then be held at the point of destination until the proper import license papers could be filled out.

The combination of restrictive local law and significant transportation barriers caused many European companies to atrophy within their country of origin. Why expand, they asked, when it was so easy to make money at home and so difficult to fight your way across the next border?

The net effect of this "fortress mentality" was economic stagnation characterized by small, inefficient plants, low investment, technological backwardness and high unemployment. For many years in the 1980's, the U.S. created more new jobs in one year than Europe had in the previous ten, even though Western Europe had a larger population than the United States.

With the kind of discouraging growth experienced by Europe over the past fifteen or twenty years, it's no wonder various aggressive European companies came to America. Here we have a huge national market with virtually no internal tariff restrictions, a very favorable political environment with relatively low taxes, a large pool of willing workers unencumbered by restrictive (European) labor laws or a history of labor/management class hatred.

On the other hand, the insular attitude of many European companies and the power concentrated in the hands of the retail trade made Europe a poor place for companies like HMG to go prospecting for business. The typical European company was oriented toward doing business in one country and that generally meant only a few hundred retail establishments. We couldn't justify the time and expense of servicing accounts that would generate a few hundred display units. Conversely, the potential clients didn't want to stand the expense of amortizing the cost of development and expensive molds over a few units.

In a way, our attitude toward Europe was the same as the typical European company toward its own business: don't invest — stagnate — don't grow.

Something had to be done, and finally it was. Seeing the enormous economic growth of Japan and the U.S., European political leaders decided to do away with virtually all the barriers that had divided (and conquered) Western Europe. They decided to outlaw all the nagging regulations that had forbidden Dutch product A from being sold in France and French product B from being sold in Italy.

Now everyone in the world has awakened to the fact that Western Europe comprises a larger market than the U.S., and that the kind of manufacturing scale we take for granted in the U.S. (and in Japan) suddenly makes sense in Europe.

Perhaps not surprisingly, some of the companies which are best positioned to capitalize upon the new "United States of Europe" are U.S. companies like IBM, Ford, Procter & Gamble and Gillette. The latter two companies are taking a category-by-category approach to Europe and are expanding virtually identical products across the continent. Gillette has even done away with its old country companies and is marketing the same product in France, Germany, England, etc.

Interestingly, Gillette's profits are up nearly 50% in real dollars since they went Pan-European.

HMG can compete and prosper in this kind of environment. The physical laws of display are the same in Europe as in the U.S. "E still equals mc²!" Now the commercial attitudes and the economies of scale in Europe are becoming similar to those in the U.S.

That's why we are aggressively expanding into Europe. We can design a display for product X in Spain and use it throughout the rest of Europe with appropriate modifications for language. As Pan-European brands and products develop, we hope to be right there offering them to consumers, following the same laws of consumer-retail interaction we've learned in the U.S.

I'm not trying to say that marketing in Europe is the same as marketing in the U.S. It isn't.

American manufacturers would slash their wrists if they had to deal with most European retailers on their terms. In some countries, even very strong brands often must pay "tribute" to the retailer at the end of the year just to stay on the shelf the following year. Then, too, there is no "Robinson-Patman" Act in Europe as there is in America. This law requires American manufacturers to offer the same terms of sale on an "equal and proportionate" basis to all retailers. In most European countries, each retailer can demand his own special deal and often does so, to the detriment of the manufacturer. Perhaps that's why in America, grocery retailers make 1% profit after tax and manufacturers make 8%. In Europe, the retailers make approximately 3% to 5%, and so do the manufacturers.

Another result of the strength of the European retailer is that private label (store) brands are a much more important feature of the consumer landscape than in the United States. European retailers swear that this is a function of better private label quality in Europe rather than the fact that they control their own shelf space as, of course, American retailers also do. Whatever the reason, store brands are much stronger in Europe, thereby complicating the lives of the manufacturers of branded goods.

Rumor has it that A&P intends to introduce a line of premium quality private label products into their U. S. stores at the urging of their German "owners." Perhaps now we'll all get to see whether higher quality private brands can compete effectively with national brands.

Another problem for manufacturers in Europe is the relative weakness and lesser availability of television advertising. It is difficult for an American marketer (or a TV viewer) to imagine just how different TV advertising is in many European countries. In Germany, for example, commercials may not appear in the context of a program. Rather, they are strung together in groups of five or six between programs. In other countries, time is rationed, if it is available at all.

Promotional laws also vary dramatically from country to country in Europe, and in no country are the laws as liberal as they are here in the U.S. For example, in France, a marketer may not give away free products, run a sweepstakes or offer a coupon good on the next purchase of the product. Why? God only knows. Just don't expect the rules to be the same as in the U.S. or, for that matter, even from country to country.

The differences among countries in Europe make possibilities for world brands, or even Pan-European brands, highly questionable, especially in food products which are so closely tied to the culture of the country. Take coffee, for example. In less than three hours, you can drive from The Netherlands to Germany and then to France, go to the coffee section of the stores in each country and find three completely different sets of brands, none of which is sold in any of the other countries.

What's more, you would find that the brands favored in each country taste somewhat different. Please do not try to convince me that a brand from any one of these countries is going to be able to invade another country and develop much of a business. It just isn't going to happen. The same can be said for a whole range of other categories, especially food and over-the-counter drugs.

But Pan-European brands (many of them American) do exist, and more Pan-European products will develop, especially in product categories outside of food.

The real message in all of this is that the world is shrinking. European companies continue to invade America, bringing their operating concepts, ideas and brands with them. The reverse is clearly true as well. American companies continue to invade Europe, bringing their operating concepts, ideas and brands with them. No one should feel threatened by this.

What do we Americans lose because Benetton (Italy) or Brooks Brothers (Great Britain) or A&P (Germany) or Food Lion (Belgium) or Lean Cuisine (Switzerland) or Dannon Yogurt (France) are successful enterprises?

How are Europeans hurt by the fact that U.S. companies own 10% of European production capacity? (IBM is the second largest exporter from West Germany after Mercedes!)

In the long run, if markets are kept open to competition, the real winners are the consumers, who get superior products at low prices, and the employees and shareholders of the companies which provide superior products.

Thirty years from now, the ownerships and employee base of most large companies will be so multi-national that no one will think about whether company X is U.S., European or Japanese. Ask yourself these questions: Is the Honda made in Marysville, Ohio, an American car or a Japanese car? Is Douwe Egberts coffee less Dutch because it reports its earnings to the Sara Lee office in Chicago?

Both of these companies will succeed or fail based upon how well they meet the needs of consumers in their market. There are no "national" or "international" customers. There are only local customers.

At HMG, we've learned that the "physics" of the transaction at retail, where a single customer stands in front of a shelf of merchandise, is basically the same all over the world. That's why we're confident that we can succeed internationally, even if that means making a counter display for a Japanese company to use in America or one for an American company to use in France.

89

CHAPTER TWELVE

Learning From (and About) Europe

As Europe has become a more attractive place for HMG to do business, we have forced ourselves to study it intensely. I have spent a lot of personal time roaming store aisles in Europe. More importantly, teams of HMG designers and researchers have gone to Europe to learn about Europe and to learn from Europe.

I would like to share some of our more important findings with you.

Let me start with the basis of all retailing... *the consumer's pocketbook.* Most of Western Europe has a lot of well-paid, well-educated workers. I was very surprised to learn that the average hourly wage in much of Europe is virtually identical to that of the U.S. This means that workers in these countries have plenty of money to spend, and employers in these countries will not benefit from cheaper labor in an economic battle with the U.S.

True, some of the countries on the edges of Western Europe (Greece, Spain, Britain, Ireland and especially Portugal) do have much lower wages than the U.S. or their sister countries in the EEC. The implications of this wage difference used to be very clear to me. I was convinced major European employers would build factories producing labor-intensive goods in these low-wage countries and "import" the products back into high-wage economies like France, Germany and Italy. Now that Eastern Europe has turned away from communism, however, I'm not so sure. These Eastern European countries have an exceptionally low wage structure with millions of well-educated workers eager to enjoy the fruits of capitalism. I don't pretend to know exactly what will happen, but I don't think the outlying Western European countries will grow quite as fast as they would have before the revolution in Eastern Europe.

The real point is this. A lot of people live in Western Europe, and most of them make excellent wages not markedly different from the U.S. In short, there are a lot of pocketbooks filled with money to spend.

A second important point is that the *distribution system* in Europe is quite different from that of the U.S. and varies significantly from country to country. From among these differences emerge certain similarities. Retailing is much more concentrated in Europe than in the U.S. That is, a few companies control a much larger percentage of the total goods sold than is the case in the U.S. Perhaps as a result, store brands are more important in Europe than in the U.S. Lastly, perhaps because of greater population density, a much larger percentage of total food volume is done in very large format stores, the so-called *hypermarkets*.

The most extreme examples of retail concentration are found in Belgium and France. In Belgium, a country roughly the size of New Jersey, 450 stores do 60% of the volume. In France, a country of nearly 50 million people, 750 stores do about 40% of the business. Most of the conventional commentary regarding this situation (including some of our own) has focused on the difficulty this presents, both to American and European manufacturers.

The standard litany goes something like this: the retailer is more powerful in Europe; he charges more to get on the shelves and stay on the shelves, and he constantly pressures you with high-quality store brands at low prices (all of this is true). As a result, the manufacturer (American, European or Martian) must approach any marketing venture in Europe with great respect for the retailer and with superior knowledge of the marketplace so that his product can keep the space he will pay so dearly to "rent" from the retailer.

But there is another implication for manufacturers which you cannot appreciate until you have walked into one of these huge European stores as a shopper. Their enormous size and kaleidoscopic variety overwhelms and confuses the shopper. In too many cases, the European hypermarket is designed for the convenience of the retail operator and not for shoppers. As a result, dozens of individual sales are lost daily; millions of dollars of sales are lost annually.

This situation represents a major opportunity for manufacturers who understand space management. When our HMG team first went into one of these huge retailers, we were struck by the chaotic jumble of products and by how repugnant it was to someone accustomed to the orderly and intelligent space usage in most U.S. mass volume retailers. At the same time, we saw that the enormous size and tremendous volume of the stores could enable manufacturers to develop customized, in-store merchandising systems that could totally replace the huge gondolas, dump bins and wire cages where most merchandise is "displayed."

I don't want to suggest that these stores are nothing but giant rummage sales with merchandise piled on the floors. That isn't true. Some sections within most hypermarkets are well conceived from the shopper's standpoint. Certainly the cosmetics sections are well done. The butcher shops and store bakeries are often well done, too. But on the whole, the stores are designed to provide low-priced answers to a mass consumer. The consumer seeking an individualized answer to her shopping needs finds the hypermarket confusing, difficult to shop and very time-consuming.

Changes are coming and fairly quickly. Some hypermarkets are dramatically upgrading their health and beauty aids sections which have been an unshoppable jumble. Even more interesting things are taking place in high-cube, fast-moving categories like paper diapers and packaged snacks.

Huge, top-loaded dump bins allow consumers to pull a package from the bottom of the chute where it is immediately replaced by the gravity-fed package resting on top of it. The entire display is efficiently loaded from the top by store personnel while shopping continues at a frenzied pace. These huge dump bins, much larger than anything regularly used in the United States, are a step in the right direction, but as currently designed, they have several problems of their own. For example, they are not clearly marked on the front so that consumers can immediately tell which variety of disposable diaper or snack they are getting.

I believe some of this confusion is deliberate on the retailer's part. European retailers certainly go to great lengths to duplicate the package design of leading branded products with their store brand products. It isn't difficult for me to believe that they would feed store brand product into the dump bins along with branded items, hoping that some consumers would buy these store brands by mistake and others would equate them in value to the national brands with which they share space.

I must admit our HMG teams were taken aback by the differences between the U.S. and European shopping experiences as represented by the European hypermarkets. Some members of our team concluded that countries in Europe had simply failed to develop a mature supermarket industry as we know it, jumping instead directly from small mom-and-pop retailers to these giant stores which are bigger than football fields and have 50 to 100 checkout stands. According to this reasoning, European retailers never went through the adjustment period of coping with multiple brands, sizes and types in a supermarket setting, so they simply weren't prepared to contend with the situation in the new hypermarkets.

Others in our group felt the jumbled, unattractive, unshoppable sections reflected the absence of strong manufacturers backed by knowledgeable space management suppliers like HMG. According to their reasoning, all of the major shelf merchandising breakthroughs in the U.S. have been driven by companies like L'eggs, Pillsbury and Noxell which, in collaboration with HMG, have shown retailers how to organize categories so that they are much more satisfying to shop (read quicker and easier).

As is often the case, both viewpoints are somewhat correct, and everyone agrees that these large European retail stores are much more difficult to shop and much less efficient for consumers and manufacturers than large U.S. supermarkets. That's the bad news.

Now for the good news — a lot of learning is going on in a lot of different places.

First, and probably most importantly, European retailers are getting a lot of direct experience in the U.S. through their ownership of stores like A&P, Food Lion, Grand Union, Shaw's, etc. The Europeans who have opened hypermarkets here in the U.S. are getting a real education about adjusting to U.S. shoppers who have spent most of their lives in well-organized, well-merchandised supermarkets. Research indicates that these consumers have told hypermarket operators in no uncertain terms about the relative difficulty in finding merchandise, fighting their way through crowded aisles, etc. We simply must believe the Europeans will apply this learning to their own European stores.

Another major factor affecting the European retailer's learning curve is the growing importance of U.S. brands and U.S. merchandising techniques. The cross fertilization of U.S.-trained managers in European companies frequently results in the manager's adapting a U.S. merchandising solution to European reality. Inevitably, each successful example breeds another because retailers can begin to see the advantages their new merchandising schemes have for them.

The last factor affecting the European retailer's learning about space management is companies like HMG. We spend time researching categories, researching shoppers and researching buying logistics at the point of sale in Europe. This research cannot be conducted in a vacuum. Much of it is done with the knowledge and collaboration of the retailer. Naturally, we often share our results with retailers as we learn from them and their customers.

In most cases, we have great credibility with the retailers because we are not perceived as someone who is trying to sell them something. We capitalize upon this attitude by positioning ourselves as disinterested "scientists" trying to develop better ways to sell more merchandise. As a result, we receive good cooperation. This helps us do our job better, it helps our clients and, of course, it helps the retailer in the long run.

As this is being written, HMG has over 100 active projects in Europe. On every project, we're educating European retailers about the importance of space management and merchandising at the point of sale. Even those developmental projects which never see the light of day will have some impact on retailers' attitudes, because they will inevitably be more sensitized to what we believe is reality.

Throughout our European experience, however, we like to believe the big winner will be our clients and, by extension, HMG. We believe we can help them understand Europe better, adjust to it better and thereby, profit from our experience.

Some of the things we have learned have surprised us, while some have merely reminded us forcefully of things we already "knew." All of our learning constantly reminds us of the reality that Europe is different from the U.S. Virtually every product moving from the U.S. to Europe will have to be carefully modified in one or more of the following key areas:

- product features
- labeling
- packaging
- name
- ad positioning

- ad execution
- media mix
- sales promotion
- price
- usage instructions

Let me share some of our more interesting discoveries with you, not because they will necessarily be of direct applicability, but because they underscore just how different Europe truly is from the United States.

Let's start with the simple area of color. All European customers interpret colors the same way. Right? Wrong! In Great Britain (as in the U.S.), a shiny black package often conveys prestige and quality. In Italy and other Mediterranean countries, black is unmistakably the color of mourning. People in those countries favor brighter colors to convey prestige or expensive taste.

Understanding nonverbal communication, such as that conveyed by color, symbols and design, is important in Europe precisely because there is no universal language. Although English is well understood by the educated elite in many European countries, it is definitely not the language with which 80% of European consumers feel comfortable. Therefore, the market can choose to communicate in a dozen or so local languages or rely more heavily on nonverbal communication such as color, shape, symbol or gesture (the famous "Charlie" pat on the fanny of her male friend is a classic of nonverbal communication).

My favorite example for understanding the difficulty of language in Europe involves just one country, Belgium, a country evenly split between French- and Flemish-speaking groups. In some areas of the country, a marketer can survive with both French and Flemish on the package. In others, it is advisable to use either one language or the other. As if that weren't bad enough, about 100,000 Belgians along the German border speak primarily German, so they are unlikely to react to communication in French or Flemish. The lesson is clear — never underestimate the importance of language barriers or the importance of communicating to consumers in the language they understand best.

Oddly enough, the power and persistence of ancient language barriers may prove most vulnerable to the newest marketing weapon, *interactive, point-of-sale devices.* Marketers can easily program these devices in multiple languages. The consumer can then choose the language with which she is most comfortable and receive a message, benefiting from the nuances of her language and culture. For this reason, we are convinced electronic, interactive, point-of-sale devices, such as our sister company, MarkitStar, developed for Noxell's Clarion cosmetics line in the U.S., have major potential in the high-traffic, multilingual European retail environment.

Another surprising aspect of marketing in Europe is the difficulty in conducting research. This difficulty exists on several different levels. First, in many European countries, marketers cannot rely upon the telephone to conduct research because large segments of the population do not own a telephone. Hence, accurate probability samples are sometimes difficult to build.

A more subtle and difficult research problem is the built-in, culturally biased answers in various countries. For example, the standard response rates to one marketing researcher's basic set of questions ("would you definitely buy, probably buy, probably not buy, definitely not buy?") vary dramatically from Southern to Northern Europe. A Southern European is more likely to give positive answers than a Northern European. Therefore, an American unfamiliar with cultural norms would be totally misled by an unusually high or low score from one country to another.

Similarly, we have learned that certain kinds of products are easier to market across various cultures than others. New technologies and fashions seem to be able to jump national and cultural boundaries relatively easily. Other products, especially food products, seem much more closely bound to culture and nationality. Some argue that the real differences in Europe are less cultural differences than social class differences. Certainly I would agree that a well-educated, upscale Italian has many things in common with a well-educated Englishman, but in the final analysis, it seems very clear that language and cultural behavior are much more deeply ingrained and much more important in many categories than are social class differences within countries.

Habits, especially eating habits, are hard to break, while new habits, especially new eating habits, are hard to establish. A fascinating study in this regard is American marketers' efforts to teach Europeans to eat cold breakfast cereals. Kellogg is slowly succeeding in teaching the very prideful French to pour milk on toasted grain. It helps that virtually all people in all European countries want to eat healthful, quick breakfasts, so Kellogg is not pushing water (or milk, as the case may be) uphill. Of course, Kellogg had to teach Americans to change their breakfast habits some eighty years ago, so the company has some reason to feel confident that, given time, patience and money, they can grow the category in Europe.

Another significant difference between American and European retailers is the relative sophistication of American retailers in the use of electronically generated, computer-driven, shelf-stocking models known as direct product profit, or DPP, models. This technique, widely understood and broadly used by U.S. retailers and manufacturers, is still in its infancy with most European retailers.

The lead U.S. retailers enjoy in this area makes it difficult for Americans to deal with a common misunderstanding that many European retailers show regarding U.S. retailing practices. Some Europeans are unwilling to accept any advice on category shelf management from Americans because they are convinced all of our stores are identical "cookie cutter" models. We have been trying to convince these Europeans that all of the scanning data we generate in the

U.S. comes in real handy in modifying shelf sets to match the extraordinary diversity of retail trading areas in many large American metro areas. I think it's safe to say that no European retailer deals with the ethnic diversity found in New York, Los Angeles, Chicago or Miami.

Certainly no European grocery retailer is as skilled in dealing with computer shelf models as any number of large U.S. manufacturers (e.g., P&G, Ralston Purina, General Foods, etc.). We (HMG and American manufacturers) are ahead of the power curve when it comes to managing category shelf space for maximum profit and consumer satisfaction on a store-by-store, neighborhood-by-neighborhood basis.

Eventually, the European retailers will come around to accepting more advice for several reasons. The evidence clearly exists that better merchandised, better presented categories are advantageous for everybody — the consumer, the manufacturer and the retailer. In the long run, the European retailer wants the same thing the American retailer wants — a store that's quick and easy to shop, and a store that has an ample supply of the items the consumer wants.

The pundits argue that the U.S. and Europe are coming closer together because of the increase in travel between the two continents and the influence of improved communications technology. I agree. But there's one factor that already unites the U.S. and European retailer — the desire for more profit!

We know that good point-of-sale merchandising, advanced, computerized, shelf management techniques and electronic, interactive, point-of-sale devices can increase retailer profit in Europe just as they do in the U.S. That's why we have opened offices in Europe. That's why we have over 100 active projects there.

CHAPTER THIRTEEN
Marks & Spencer Meets HMG

Someone once said that all progress is made by "unreasonable" men, because reasonable men adjust to their surroundings while unreasonable men rebel against them and produce "progress."

At HMG, we've discovered a similar irony. "Long-term happiness requires short-term discomfort." That's because, in the long run, people are happy only if they are learning, growing and expanding; yet, in the short-term, you can't learn, grow or expand as a person or a business unless you expose yourself to the discomforts of new ideas and new situations.

We relearn this lesson every year, and we learned it one year in what turned out to be a very pleasant way.

HMG Met Marks & Spencer

Marks & Spencer is one of the great companies in the world. They dominate retailing in the United Kingdom the way no one company does in the U.S. Every week, 14 million people walk into their 250+ stores in the U.K. They control 40% of all the underwear sold in the U.K., 20% of all hosiery, etc. Their flagship "Marble Arch" store is in the Guinness Book of Records for the most volume per square foot.

That's the good news. The bad news, as far as manufacturers are concerned, is that everything in the store is sold under one brand name, St Michael. That means that any manufacturer who wants to sell to Marks & Spencer must design their product to meet Marks & Spencer's exacting specifications, produce it to those specs and put

Marks & Spencer's St Michael label on it.

To manage this unusual system, M&S has over 4,000 employees in its headquarters on Baker Street in London. The first time I saw M&S headquarters I was taken aback. It's an old building with all these people working in large, open areas sitting at hundreds of desks packed against one another. It reminded me of a hive of bees with everyone working separately, but somehow working with a common purpose, to get thousands of high-quality products from hundreds of manufacturers shipped to the far-flung M&S empire in the right colors, sizes and amounts, on time.

Redesigning literally thousands of products may seem unnecessary, unreasonable and terribly complicated, but M&S makes it work.

HMG met Marks & Spencer through our long association with the Sara Lee Hosiery Division (known to the consuming public as Hanes and L'eggs). The simple story is that L'eggs wanted to sell its products through Marks & Spencer and succeeded. The real story is the courtship and marriage of two great cultures which overcame their prejudices and pride to find true love. In the process, we learned a lot, made new friends and had one hell of a good time.

HMG Played Matchmaker

The whole adventure started with Weldon Schenck who heads Sara Lee's European operation from his base in Paris. Weldon was absolutely determined to find a way to work with Marks & Spencer. After many long hours of frustration, days of doubt and a week or two of "the hell with this," Weldon provided the calm determination to win over the single most important account in the U.K.

One of the first things Weldon did was to give HMG the responsibility for designing the packaging, the point-of-sale material and the merchandising program. We also played goodwill ambassador and interpreter when the two cultures seemed bent on self-destruction.

The whole process involved a tremendous amount of hard work, transatlantic travel, midnight phone calls and long dinners relearning the old truth that "the English and the Americans are two peoples separated by a common language."

Part III - Chapter Thirteen

Simple example: we call pantyhose "pantyhose." The English call them "tights," which, of course, has a decidedly different meaning to an American.

But that wasn't all that was different. The Marks & Spencer folks were convinced that English women (their customers) wanted a specific fit and feel to their tights. So, right out of the box, they politely insisted that L'eggs be redesigned (and therefore, manufactured differently) for Marks & Spencer.

After some hesitation, the Sara Lee folks agreed for several good reasons. First, they wanted the business. Second, they were totally confident they could manufacture any hosiery anybody could possibly conceive. Third, they were certain, based on years of intensive research, that Marks & Spencer would end up mandating a design virtually identical to what L'eggs was currently making. After all, their product had been proven in use by millions of customers, and its design had been proven in literally dozens of "blind" research tests.

That's when Sara Lee got its first culture shock. The Marks & Spencer executives calmly announced that they did not believe in American-style consumer research. Their idea of consumer research is to design the best possible product, offer it at the lowest possible price in the store and wait to see if customers buy. If they do, the company wins. If they don't, the company loses. Their reasoning is simple — the best research tool is the cash register.

The Sara Lee Folks Were Horrified

Raised in the classical, disciplined environment of American marketing, their product development path is to design, test with consumers, re-design, re-test, sell in a test market area, re-design some more, study results and then go national.

The Marks & Spencer formula is much simpler. It's something like design, re-design, go national. This works real well for them because they own the stores.

As is often the case in situations like this, a constructive compromise was reached. The Sara Lee people let the Marks & Spencer folks do the initial stipulation on design specification based upon their knowledge of the British market, M&S price points, etc. Then the

Sara Lee folks did consumer testing as a "disaster check." Everyone learned something from the process. Marks & Spencer came away with a healthy respect for what can be learned through a disciplined process. Sara Lee learned how a different culture reacts to a different package and product design.

While all this design and testing was going on, HMG was going full speed ahead on the retail presentation aspects of the program. During this process, we came to know, respect and, much to everyone's surprise, downright enjoy some of the key people at M&S, especially Barry Maisel and the legendary John Poppleton.

Barry Maisel held a typically British title at M&S. He was a "senior selector." Barry is a good-spirited Brit who, in our first meeting, mentioned that he "worked hard and played hard." (Barry is now managing director of HMG U.K.)

For Barry, working hard means being at his desk from 7 in the morning until 8 at night. Playing hard means being in restaurants every other waking moment. He especially loves combining "hard work" and "hard play," as I have learned over countless business breakfasts, lunches and dinners.

I remember well the first time I scheduled a breakfast meeting in London with Barry. He readily agreed until I suggested we eat at my hotel. "Oh, no," he said, "I know a better place." And so, early the next morning, I trooped over to another hotel. The minute I walked in I understood why it was Barry's favorite. It was London's only "all you can eat for one price" breakfast buffet. Here was a "senior selector" who got his money's worth starting with breakfast.

From the outset, we "got on" well with the M&S staff, partly because we saw this project as an excellent opportunity to learn from some very smart, highly successful people. It's amazing how well you can "get on" with people when you're open to learning from them.

Oddly enough, our good relationship with the M&S folks began with a disaster. The English had come to "the colonies" for their first meeting at Sara Lee Hosiery headquarters in Winston-Salem, North Carolina. The meeting went poorly. I am convinced it was because the English couldn't stand all the strange fried food the southerners at Sara Lee shoved at them. (Maisel still blanches at the mention of grits.) Whatever the reason, the meetings were not successful. Following the initial meeting in Winston-Salem, the M&S representatives were scheduled to visit our offices in New York. The Sara Lee folks called in a mild panic. "Mike, we didn't have a good meeting. Do whatever you can to save the day."

The first thing I did was to marshal our team for an extra special presentation. I had our people work all night for two nights, drawing sketches, building models, preparing for the morning presentation.

The next thing I did was to schedule a good meal for Barry and Judy Cohen, at Le Bernardin, a fine French restaurant. Barry seemed greatly relieved to move from grits to bordelaise and bearnaise. Our friendship flourished over the *foie gras*.

The next day, we took Barry and his team through a presentation with lots of "toys" (sketches, mock-ups, a model, etc.). The Marks & Spencer team was captivated. While we were busy playing down our work ("they're preliminary ideas, etc."), Barry was busy trying to cram the material into his briefcase. He was determined to take it all back to London. "These are great," he said while dismantling our presentation. He even called London immediately after the meeting to tell his counterparts about our work.

Then we had an incredible stroke of good luck. By coincidence, the day of the M&S presentation was the day of our annual Caribbean beach party at HMG. We close the office after lunch and go down to another floor which is converted into a Caribbean beach. The party is an excuse to raise money for great organizations which help runaway kids.

Remember, we're in the display business, so when we want to create an indoor beach, we create one complete with sand, palm trees, water, etc.

Since the M&S folks were around, we invited them to the "beach party." When we made our entrance, the place was a madhouse. Our employees were dressed in beach attire, and all sorts of games were going on, including a dunking game complete with ball, target, a tub of water and various HMG employees willing to be soaked for charity. Many employees were lining up for the chance to dunk our chief financial officer or any number of the attractive young women in our office. The CFO was the crowd favorite since dunking turns out to be a socially acceptable form of torture.

Little did I know that the English (who have an undeserved reputation for stuffiness) are positively balmy about games of all sorts, from potato sack races to water-filled balloon tosses. When they saw the HMG employees running around in bathing suits on the ninth floor of an office building in the heart of Manhattan, they felt right at home. It was as though we had imported a little bit of England to New York.

And so, surrounded by hot dog carts, sand, dunking machines and a Caribbean steel drum band, Marks & Spencer met the real HMG. They loved it. They met our creative director, our accounting people, our model builders, our engineers and, when he wasn't gasping for air, our CFO.

Several weeks later, I learned that Barry and his people had told everyone at M&S about this crazy American company which "worked hard and played hard, just like we do." For months thereafter, whenever I met someone within Marks & Spencer, they would say, "Oh, yes, the beach party man."

Word even reached Weldon Schenck in Paris, because a few days later, he left a message on my voice mail that said, "Mike, thanks for saving the day."

The beach party cemented our relationship with M&S. We began to work closely with them, and through this experience, developed a great respect and affection for the wonderful institution that is M&S.

They work incredible hours, seldom stopping before 8 or 9 at night and then move on to grand dinners. Their hospitality knows no bounds.

I remember one particular occasion when they invited me to dinner, knowing full well that I am a smoker. One of the best restaurants in London is a place called Chez Nico, the kind of restaurant where the chef doesn't want people to drink, and certainly not smoke, because it interferes with their palates. Had they simply told me, "Mike there's no smoking at this restaurant," it would have been fine, but instead, they called the chef, and with some difficulty, arranged for a private room where I could smoke.

Of course, I was unaware of all this and found it fascinating to see no ashtrays on the table. Assuming there was no smoking in this area, I did not smoke. Finally, after 30 or 40 minutes at the table, someone said, "Mike, did you give up smoking?"

I said, "No."

They asked why I wasn't smoking, and I responded that I wasn't aware that smoking was permitted. They said, "Oh, yes, we arranged this room so you could smoke here." We got an ashtray, and I did light up a cigarette, along with six other people at the table. They really liked it and probably couldn't wait to tell their friends that they were among the very few people who ever went to Chez Nico and smoked. By the way, the food is excellent, and I do recommend it highly.

On another occasion, Barry invited my wife and me to his home to meet his wife (who also works for M&S) and their two lovely children. Barry picked us up at our hotel because "we're going to have tea first." You can put me down for ignorant, because I had no idea that "tea" (at least Barry's idea of it) included all sorts of goodies such as salmon, cake, candy, etc. We enjoyed a very long "tea time," squeezed in a quick visit to the Maisel manse and moved rapidly to dinner. Around midnight, we returned to the hotel. I felt like one of those huge, inflated animals in the Macy's Thanksgiving Day Parade. One thing about Barry — he takes your stomach to places it's never been before.

During our long working hours and innumerable dinners, Barry and the rest of the M&S team had been preparing me to meet John Poppleton, one of the most important executives in the company. John is in charge of advertising, public relations and various other aspects of Marks & Spencer's public persona.

Poppleton may very well be the busiest person on Planet Earth. His time is scheduled months in advance in five-minute increments! This means that a manufacturer who wants to do business with one of the largest accounts in the United Kingdom gets five minutes to make his case with John Poppleton. What's worse, he's got months to worry about this highly important, five-minute call.

My five minutes were scheduled (10:55 to 11:00), and at the appointed tick of the clock, I was ushered into Poppleton's office with

Barry Maisel, who seemed more nervous than I.

Unbeknownst to Barry, I had decided on an unusual ploy. When I walked into the office, I walked directly over to Poppleton, stuck out my hand and said, "Mr. Poppleton, it's a pleasure to meet you. I don't want to waste any more of your time today. When you have more time, I would love to get together with you." With that, I turned on my heel and began to walk out on one of the most important people in the U.K. and the busiest man on the planet.

If Barry Maisel hadn't already begun to understand that I was somewhat unusual, he probably would have had a heart attack on the spot. Fortunately, John Poppleton saved me and Barry. "Wait a minute," he said. "Come in." I returned to his desk, and we began to chat. Forty-five minutes later, he gave me a book about the history of Marks & Spencer with a personalized inscription, "To a newfound friend... Mike." He signed it, "John Poppleton."

That initial meeting with John led to others which helped me better to understand him and Marks & Spencer. I found Poppleton to be every bit as smart as everyone had said (brilliant is a better word), and I found him to be incredibly hardworking. But his reputation for being somewhat short and even a little gruff simply was not borne out in my experience.

Like virtually all of the people at M&S, he turned out to be very considerate and generous. One evening, after a long day of presentation to the M&S board, John Poppleton took my wife and me to dinner. During the conversation, my wife made a passing remark about the British Fashion Awards presentation being held the next evening. Poppleton glanced up from his soup and asked her if she would like to go. Judy was a little embarrassed that she had broached the subject, but you could tell she really did want to go. Poppleton said, "Judy, it's not a problem. We always have lots of tickets to things like this. I can find you one." With that, Judy beamed and allowed as how she'd love to go. The next day, a ticket magically arrived along with directions, a program, etc.

Later that evening, Judy returned from the show. Not only had she loved the presentation, she had sat three rows from Princess Diana. John Poppleton had made a friend for life.

Meanwhile, back at M&S, the Howard Marlboro team was trying to make the Marks & Spencer management friends for life. We had arrived at a critical juncture in our relationship. After all the work in Winston-Salem and London between the operating managements of both M&S and Sara Lee, we needed to get two critical policy issues past the M&S top management.

One was the name of the product and the other was in-store presentation. As I mentioned, every product sold in Marks & Spencer is sold under one label, St Michael. This presented something of a problem for Sara Lee since they have a policy against making private label merchandise. At first glance, this situation had all the ingredients for several world-class "Maalox moments," with visions of the executives of each company strutting about, preening themselves and stopping only long enough to read from the corporate stone tablets.

Instead, the working groups from both companies adopted a very sensible, practical approach. "Let's find a way to satisfy both policies." After several sessions, the Sara Lee folks were willing to acknowledge that the products they intended to sell in M&S were different from other L'eggs products sold elsewhere. The products were, in fact, "made especially for M&S." For their part, the M&S people were willing to recognize that the L'eggs brand name and in-store presentation were so unique that any attempt to call products something else would probably confuse and possibly even anger shoppers.

The "grand compromise" was to use the L'eggs logo but add the description, "for St Michael." This may seem simple and obvious to you, but neither company had ever done such a thing. In fact, it took a vote of the M&S board to depart from policy and put "L'eggs for St Michael" in the store.

I always will remember the final presentation to M&S top management, including its chairman, Lord Rayner. The presentation took place in the M&S boardroom which was all dark oak. Everyone sat in these incredible wooden chairs behind a huge English oak table with the ghosts of English retailing history staring down from the walls ready to veto your presentation.

The boardroom reeked of tradition. Little did we know that part of British business tradition was to limit access to the boardroom to the chosen few. As a result of this typically British business practice, few of the thousands of employees of Marks & Spencer, including some relatively highly placed executives, had ever been in the company's boardroom. When some of the group who had worked with us on the "L'eggs for St Michael" project found out that we were going to make our presentation in the hallowed boardroom, many began jockeying for the opportunity to sit in.

When the presentation was over, I learned why it had gone so well. It seems that many of the members of the M&S management group had assumed we would have the attitude that other vendors had brought to M&S. This attitude can best be summarized as "everything you people are doing is wrong; adopt our recommendation on store design, fixturing, etc., and your sales will double." M&S correctly sees this as a blatant attempt to sell them something with little or no respect for M&S tradition or consumers.

Much to their surprise, our approach was exactly the opposite. Our opening shot was simple. "You have excellent fixturing which is clearly working very well for you. We would never presume to come in here and fix something which is not broken."

You could almost feel everyone in the room relax. Then we said, "But we do have a lot of experience in selling this category, so let us show you how we would adapt your basic fixturing to sell L'eggs for St Michael." We proceeded to show the results of our long collaboration with both the Sara Lee and M&S working groups.

The net effect on the M&S management committee was very positive. They deeply appreciated our respect for their fixturing system. At the same time, they were captivated by the improvements we had incorporated into our adaptation.

One other thing helped our presentation. The English genuinely love Americans. I don't know whether it is our quaint accent, the fact that Winston Churchill's mother was American or that we have fought side by side in two terrible wars. My own theory is that the British see Americans as innocent, younger brothers unburdened by the negative baggage of England's stifling class system. The British know we Americans put the highest value on talent and hard work and not on a 500-year-old title. They respect us deeply for that, and a part of them wants to be like us.

They expect Americans to be somewhat irreverent, and far from being offended, they find it downright endearing. I certainly did my part to reaffirm the American reputation for bantering good humor when I was introduced to Lord Rayner, chairman of M&S.

It never occurred to me to call anyone Lord Something, so I automatically blurted out, "Mr. Lord, I'm so pleased to meet you." My American co-workers winced, but I thought sure I saw a smile flicker in Poppleton's eyes. Lord Rayner himself laughed out loud as he stretched out his hand to greet me. The tension of the moment evaporated, and for the rest of the presentation, I addressed the chairman as Mr. Lord to the evident delight of everyone, including the Lord himself.

We got the order — not only that order, but several more.

It seems the management of Marks & Spencer realized from our presentation just what a disciplined approach to space management could mean to their stores.

Our relationship with Marks & Spencer grows broader and deeper on a monthly basis. We enjoy the M&S people, and we love the spirit of the company.

Most importantly, we learned from them. We learned lessons we are applying to a growing business in Europe. Stated simply, we learned that many of the rules for in-store marketing in Europe are identical to the U.S. rules, but that some aspects of the European culture and shopping experience are so different that you must adapt or die in the marketplace.

A few weeks later, I was driving to Newark Airport on my way to North Carolina when the car phone rang, and through the magic of modern communication, I was connected to Gerry Hodes, an executive with Marks & Spencer Foods. Gerry requested that we get involved in designing and presenting to Marks & Spencer how Marks & Spencer Foods should look. This meant we should look at everything from the signs to the typography to the colors to the packaging to the store layouts and the fixturing — a real corporate communications project.

Now you must understand that corporate communications is a field unto itself, populated with famous designers and other big-name talent. For HMG even to be requested to submit a proposal on this was incredible to me, but it was also appetizing. What made it so appetizing was that here was a foremost British company, number one in name recognition, asking HMG to participate in this tremendous undertaking.

I told Gerry Hodes that we'd be delighted to do it, and the way we worked it out was that for an initial fee, we would come up with recommendations. Everyone thought that I was crazy, but we did it and made our presentation with tremendous raves to an audience consisting of the main Food Board, including its chairman, Alan Smith.

One amusing incident that took place at the main presentation grew out of the fact that we made up not only the packaging, the colors and all the other things that go along with such presentations, but also the icing on the cake — we created what we called *The Store of the Future*. I went into this great monologue about how Marks & Spencer can take the high road, and this store of the future that does not yet exist, this store of the future that will lead retailing to new levels, this store of the future that will make it easier for consumers to shop, easier for Marks & Spencer to maintain, etc., this store that some day will come to fruition, will be the brainchild of Marks & Spencer. And I made the analogy of a Roman coliseum where, in the middle, everything is low, and it builds up to the sides, and where the audience, if they were standing in the center of the Roman coliseum, could look around and see every other person in the audience. But because this is a store, the people standing in the middle would see every product since the heights vary and go from low to high against the wall.

Well, one of the members of the board got so excited that he said, "My God, this is absolutely incredible. Where can I go and see this store of the future?"

There was a moment of silence as everyone looked at this person, and all of a sudden, someone from Marks & Spencer said, "But... don't you understand? This is the store of the future — it doesn't exist. This will be our store."

Well to top it off, I sent a letter to Marks & Spencer after the presentation was over telling them that I had found the store of the future. It was located in Chicago, off Michigan Avenue.

This really dramatizes how involved people can get in a presentation, and it also shows that our business does have a sense of humor.

Every day we learn a little more about blending unique European situations with in-store marketing. As a result, we're expanding the boundaries of the science of in-store marketing.

And we're growing our business. Our 100 projects in Europe are serviced by offices in London, Rotterdam and Paris.

One of the hidden benefits of this European effort is that what we learn over there can also be applied in the U.S. The best example is the experience we've gained in the European hypermarkets. I am convinced that some of the ideas we've developed for that unique channel of distribution can be effectively adapted for the very different U.S. supermarket.

We also have this great idea about holding beach parties in supermarkets all over America. The consumers get to dunk the store manager!

PART IV
A Business Handbook

CHAPTER FOURTEEN
What's the Matter with Business?

Every now and then at a social gathering, someone will spot me as one who works with "big business" and will ask the question, "What's the matter with business?"

Usually, the question is asked in one of two contexts: immediately after some Japanese company has scored a much publicized coup, or when an established American company gets into trouble and announces a product recall, a big quarterly loss or bankruptcy.

If I know anything about the subject, I have a tendency to answer the question with a specific response directly related to the incident in question. When I reflect on the number of times questions like this have been asked over the past five years, I realize that the questioner is often seeking a more general, perhaps I should say a more reflective response than I have been giving.

I am tempted to echo the arguments of many academicians who denounce the short-term management styles of American business "leadership." As everyone knows, eventually the long term becomes the short term, and if you haven't prepared for it, you lose.

I am also tempted to point out that foreign firms are operating within financial systems, accounting systems and cultures which have different expectations, requirements and behavioral patterns. It would take more time and frankly, a more detailed knowledge of these factors than I have, in order to provide answers worth your while.

And besides that, most American business leaders can't really do very much about many of these issues. So, instead of lamenting the high savings rates in Japan or the low return rates accepted by German investors, I'd like to focus on things we can do and on problems I do know something about from my personal experience.

If I had to identify what's wrong with American business, I'd choose these factors:

- The Pontius Pilate Syndrome.
- Uriah Heep Regnant.
- Executive Insulation.
- The Tyranny of Democracy.
- "Rain Man" Redux.

The Pontius Pilate Syndrome

The *Pontius Pilate Syndrome* is shorthand for washing your hands of the product you're selling. Virtually all successful businesses are started by people who love the product or service they're selling. They live, eat and sleep their product.

As businesses grow and "professional" management takes over, that zealous "love of product" quality gets overwhelmed by balance sheets, personnel policies, pension plans and all the other trappings of success.

No one cares about the product or service that built the building, that funded everyone's profit sharing or that paid for the corporate jet.

Talk to an entrepreneur about his business and the discussion will center around his product, his dog food, his cat box filler, her dress line. Talk to most corporate executives about their companies, and the discussion will center around stock prices, personnel problems and tax rulings.

The real challenge to American corporate leadership is to instill the love of product throughout the organization, to make everyone feel personally responsible for quality or service the way the founder so obviously did. It starts at the top. If employees sense that management doesn't care, I guarantee you they won't care.

Let me tell you two stories of companies that have managed to instill that love of product.

One is Sara Lee, a long-time and highly valued client of Howard

Marlboro. Years ago, Consolidated Foods (now known as Sara Lee Corporation) bought The Kitchens of Sara Lee, a baker of very high quality frozen foods. It would have been easy after a while for corporate management to cut corners, change the formula, increase the margins ("the consumer can't tell the difference"). Instead, whenever a new product was about to be introduced, it was subjected to the "Charlie Test." The product was tasted by Charlie Lubin, the founder of the company. If it failed the Charlie test, it wasn't sold to the public.

Charlie Lubin died a few years ago, but the "Charlie Test" remains in place as the ultimate method of *institutionalizing the love of product*. Everyone in the building understands that if it doesn't measure up to a high standard, we don't put our name on it.

Lots of people have Federal Express stories, but my favorite was told to me by a friend who sent a letter using the "two-hour guaranteed delivery" system (Zap Mail), which Fed Ex was offering at that time. After an appropriate waiting period, he called the recipient only to find that the letter had not arrived despite Fed Ex's guarantee. He called Fed Ex about the problem. Thereafter, every <u>30 minutes</u> he received a call from a special Federal Express employee updating him on their efforts to find and deliver the letter.

Finally, about four hours after he had sent the original message, he received a phone call from Memphis headquarters. A voice came on, obviously over a speaker phone. "We found your letter and delivered it 30 minutes ago. We've just come from Mr. Smith's office (Fred Smith, founder and president of Federal Express). The entire Quality Control team is here because we have to report foul-ups like this to him. We uncovered a flaw in our procedure that caused the problem. We're sorry. It won't happen again."

My friend will never trust any package delivery company as much as Federal Express, because he's convinced the employees must face Fred Smith every time they foul up. Fred Smith (whom I have never met) has managed to communicate a love of service throughout his organization. Everyone knows he cares, and because he does, his employees do.

I would be the first to admit it's easier to communicate love of product when the founding entrepreneur is still sitting in the corner office. But that isn't the point. Before a corporate executive can communicate love of product, he must first believe in it himself. Unfortunately, too many of today's executives don't love their product or their service. Too many, in fact, are ashamed to be associated with something as mundane as a drain cleaner or cake mix. Too many have played Pontius Pilate, washing their hands of the product so they can focus on a balance sheet. And we know how many consumers care about a balance sheet, don't we?

Uriah Heep Regnant

The Pontius Pilate Syndrome has been reinforced by a second major problem, the *regnancy of Uriah Heep*, the numbers-driven, accounting-educated, cost-conscious, by-the-book MBA type.

No firm can do without an accounting and finance function, but no one starts a business by hiring six accountants. The first principle of business is that you must sell something to someone before you need someone to keep count of your winnings. Businesses start with a product or service idea and a salesman, often the individual who had the idea in the first place.

Unfortunately, many businesses follow a development pattern that sees them become more and more control oriented. The surest symptom of this syndrome is the vast expansion of the control/accounting function. Too often, the expansion of the control function is quickly followed by mountains of computer-generated reports which offer lots of data and little information. I once had a very successful entrepreneur tell me, "I didn't know how hard it was to make money until I started getting all these reports." The point is, he made an absolute fortune by focusing on product superiority and customer service. Twenty years later, all his time was being spent immersed in reports that were largely unnecessary, irrelevant or incomprehensible.

The next steps, beyond the dozens of accounting types and the hundreds of pages of printouts, are cost-cutting campaigns aimed at the product that built the business. A nibble here, a nibble there, and in four or five years, the product has been cost-improved into market inferiority. This is especially the case with companies which have gone through LBO's. Great products like Del Monte's fruit cocktail and Eckrich smoked sausage simply aren't the same products they were ten years ago. Someone decided to take out a few cherries this year, an apricot next year, etc., all in the name of increased margin ("the consumer can't tell the difference").

Don't get me wrong. There is a place for cost improvement campaigns. Good accountants can make a valuable contribution to any business. But in the long run, a company is better off run by Willy Loman, the salesman/marketer, than by Uriah Heep, the clerk/ accountant. That's because the salesman is the man in the arena; he's the man with his finger on the pulse of the consumer; he's the man with the best chance of responding to the marketplace—the ultimate judge of profit and loss.

Executive Insulation

How does it happen, you might ask, that top executives get divorced from their product and their marketplace? The answer is *executive insulation*, a major disease infecting corporate America.

Let me explain by citing a classic example of an "executive" who isn't suffering from insulation — Jim Koch, founder and president of Samuel Adams Brewery in Boston. Mr. Koch was consumed by the desire to brew a great beer. After the typical entrepreneurial scramble for investors, he developed his product and decided to sell it by going from bartender to bartender in Boston with his own sample "six pack." He had to face these bartenders while they tasted his beer for the first time. He felt the thrill of getting an order and the agony of rejection. He was not insulated from marketplace reality. His product has been extremely successful.

Contrast Mr. Koch with the president of Kraft back in the late 1970's. He made ceremonial visits to the field to look at Kraft's products. Everyone knew when he and his retinue were coming, so the local sales management arranged a "milk run" of stores that had been worked over by a horde of local Kraft salesmen before the big boss ever set foot in them. These staged milk runs were an open secret within the company. Of course, no one bothered to tell me this

116

when HMG was summoned to Chicago to present ideas on space management.

I appeared for the presentation and was ushered into a huge conference room. I was surprised to find all the top brass of Kraft at the meeting. My associate and I began by talking about the principles of space management. Then I got up and said something like, "I can understand why this issue is receiving top management attention because Kraft does have a major problem." Well, the room got as quiet as a morgue. No one looked one way or the other, and several of the Kraft executives stared at their feet.

Finally the president piped up. "What problem, Mr. Wahl?" Fortunately, we had done a photo audit of several Kraft categories and I had actual pictures of their products in real stores (not "milk run" stores). I turned off the lights and began to show the Kraft top brass the truth. It was a very painful ten minutes. No one said a word. Then when I turned the lights back on, the president thanked me and asked if my associate and I would mind leaving the room for a moment.

As we were sitting outside the conference room, I asked my associate who had set up the meeting, "Did I say something wrong in there?"

"No," he assured me.

About ten minutes later, the door opened and the president came out. He apologized for ending the meeting so abruptly and indicated that they would be calling us. In two weeks, we got a call from Kraft, and the caller explained what had happened. Our photo audit had been a tremendous revelation to the president, who had only seen "milk run" stores for years. When he saw our slides, he became incensed over the true condition of his shelves and over his own insulation.

No one had had the guts to tell him that he was insulated because he had signaled in a hundred little ways that he wanted to be insulated. In this respect, he shares a desire, or a disease, as I prefer to call it, which is rampant in American business.

Too many executives have a four-point plan for failure:

- Surround yourself with a large staff of sycophants.

- Avoid contact with real consumers.

- Never step into a real store.

- Never talk to a supplier or vendor.

Too often, these executives end up managing a fantasy world instead of a real company.

The Tyranny of Democracy

The only thing worse than a company with an insulated top executive is one which suffers from the *tyranny of democracy.*

Several years ago, American business was afflicted by "psycho-babble" types singing the praises of "participatory management." This "new style" was supposed to lead to better decisions, happier employees, better retention rates, higher profits and a lowering of skin cancer. I must admit that I do like some aspects of "participatory management." It does have certain advantages, even if it doesn't cure cancer. Even though I am "the Boss," I don't know everything, so it helps to let people I am paying to think do so out loud so I can reap something from my investment in them.

The problems begin when a pathological form of participatory management develops. We call it "a democracy." Business is not a democracy. Successful businesses are designed to give some people more "votes" than others. These people are older, wiser, more experienced, more sensitive, more creative, etc. They're called "bosses." Really bad companies don't have bosses — they have democracies.

For complex reasons, some companies suffer from a compulsion to let everyone participate in virtually every decision. They spend hours seeking "input" from individuals who lack the competence or the experience to comment on anything, much less the problem at hand. The best analogy I can come up with is an operating room where the surgeon would somehow feel compelled to seek advice on a complex procedure from the charwoman. There's obviously nothing wrong, and a whole lot right, with seeking the opinion of an informed expert. In fact, the highly regarded "gurus" of the Total Quality Management movement, like Philip Crosby and Dr. W. Edwards Deming, teach that

118

it's the person on the firing line, such as the individual machine operator in a factory, rather than the bosses, who really knows best how improvements can be made in the work process. If this kind of input into day-to-day operations can be tapped and institutionalized, so much the better. But in a crisis, you just don't have the time to waste soliciting advice, or worse, waiting for agreement from everyone in a specific group.

The key point here is time. Everyone in business spends time talking about this asset and that asset, but the most important asset any business has is time. Why? There are two reasons: time goes away, and it can never be retrieved. It is a constantly depleting asset which must be used to its fullest every second of every day. Moreover, if you move quickly enough and beat a competitor to the marketplace with idea X or product Y, you will get the lion's share of the profit available in the category, and you will get it for years, possibly forever. I know of no business category where the first guy in with the right product, properly supported, hasn't escaped with most of the profit.

But it is precious time that the tyranny of democracy wastes! And it wastes that time primarily in that hallowed business ritual, the meeting. I will not go so far as to say that all business meetings are a waste of time. Clearly, they are not. Meetings with clients, suppliers and other "outsiders" are often extremely valuable.

It's the internal meetings, the interdepartmental meetings, that are killers because they waste so much time with everyone compromising and playing democracy.

I wish American business would schedule meetings with the care normally used for disarming explosive devices or choosing a wife. Everyone would be a lot better off. But most businessmen love meetings. They break the monotony of the day, obviate the need to do real work and often provide entertainment, camaraderie, new jobs, etc. Unfortunately, they also create the conditions for the tyranny of democracy.

There is something about meeting etiquette that requires everyone to speak, often at length, often irrelevantly.

There is also something about meeting etiquette that requires agreement, even where none exists or none is necessary. (What difference does it make if the operating room charwoman wants to leech my wounds?)

In a truly pathological situation, the tyranny of democracy can deteriorate into the tyranny of the malevolent or the merely stupid.

The two best (or worst) examples both involve a particular retailer who is famous for wall-to-wall meetings. One executive shared his calendar with a friend of mine and revealed he had a meeting scheduled every hour of every day for an entire month.

"When do you work?" my friend asked.

"This is work," the executive replied.

"Oh, no it isn't," my friend countered.

This company had a senior executive who was famous for bad meeting etiquette. He would always find something to criticize or some issue with which to disagree. Countless hours were wasted by everyone looking for consensus with an individual who was actually a bully. After years of terrorizing the company, disrupting meetings and exploiting democracy, he was caught in some shady dealings with an outside supplier and canned. He should have been dismissed years earlier for democracy abuse!

This same company tolerated incredible delays in a project because an executive without any direct interest in the project kept raising tangential issues.

The tyranny of democracy demanded this executive get a hearing. In fact, he got four different hearings because no one would stand up and tell him his opinion was insufficient to delay this project. Finally, the supplier became so exasperated with the retailer that he withdrew his offer and left them without access to the service they desired.

"Rain Man" Redux

A truly extreme form of the tyranny of democracy is what I call *"Rain Man" Redux*. You remember the "Rain Man," an idiot savant capable of extraordinary feats of mental agility in a specific area even though he could not perform simple, everyday activities.

In some companies, management has become so lazy or stupid or cowardly that they allow decisions to be made by employees who lack the training or capabilities to make an intelligent choice. Management justifies its abdication on the grounds of participatory democracy, good, long-range, people-development policies, or on mysticism. ("They are closer to the marketplace than I. They know their territory, etc.")

One wonders what decisions, if any, management reserves for itself in these companies (the menu at lunch?). One wonders what management believes its job to be in a company like this. Perhaps they should just call a meeting of all the Rain Men in the company, hand them the keys to the executive washroom and leave for an early round of golf.

But, of course, that's what's already happened.

Please do not believe this occurs in every company. It doesn't. For every company where this does happen, there are three where the following scene is played out as it was for a friend of mine:

"I've heard your arguments. I've thought about this subject a lot. You may be right, but I don't think so. And because I'm the boss, we're going to do it my way."

Part IV

CHAPTER FIFTEEN
Time

A decade or so ago at year's end, before throwing out the used appointment calendar for the year just passed, I began thumbing through it, reliving the year day by day, stopping to smile over a triumph or reflect on a tragedy. For reasons unclear to me, I have always been consumed by the passage of time, so the opportunity to observe my own life passing before my eyes was fascinating in the extreme.

Ever since that first "life review," I have spent every December 31st reviewing the previous year's calendar of events. I have even developed a concept similar to accountants' "sources and uses of funds" that you see included in the annual reports of most corporations. I call it the "uses of time" concept. I think it's a very important concept for a few, simple reasons.

Time is the most precious commodity on earth. Once it's gone, it's gone. It cannot be recaptured, re-used, retrieved or recycled.

Time is a hard, but fair, democratic taskmaster. Every person on earth gets only 60 minutes in every hour, 24 hours in every day. The wealthiest man on earth cannot buy a 61-minute hour or a 25-hour day. Conversely, the poorest man on earth gets the same 60-minute hour that God gives the Sultan of Brunei.

In life and in business, the person who uses time wisely winds up wealthy, perhaps not materially wealthy, but wealthy nonetheless.

In business, time is at once the most valuable and undervalued of all assets. Valuable because being first with a product, a service or an improvement therein, is disproportionately valuable. In fact, in most business categories, the leading brand or company is the one which invented the product or service decades ago.

But time is undervalued, too, because so few executives are forced to quantify the value of time except when it comes to negotiating a salary rate for hourly employees or haggling over an interest rate on a loan (after all, an interest rate is the value bankers assign to letting you have the use of their money over time).

One thing executives rarely do is quantify the value of their own time, the one asset over which they have considerable, if not perfect, control. A friend told me a story which illustrates this point perfectly.

It seems that in the early 1960's, a $250,000-a-year vice president at P&G dropped a pencil under the table during a meeting with a group of engineers. Being your basic, conservative, responsible, waste-not-want-not Cincinnatian, the executive stopped the meeting to grope under the table for his lost pencil. It took him thirty seconds to find the prodigal pencil.

One of the engineers began to calculate furiously during the lengthy groping. When the executive regained his pencil and his composure, the calculating engineer began to muse out loud. "According to the annual report, you make $250,000 a year. Assuming 250 work days a year, you make $1,000 a day or about $125/hour or a little over $2 a minute. If my calculations are correct, you just spent $1 of the shareholders' money to recapture a $.25 pencil. The next time you drop one, just ask me for a new one. A minute of your time is more valuable than that pencil." Everyone in the room was convulsed with laughter including the VP, and just to show you that humor is valued within P&G, the young engineer who made the revealing calculation was himself named a VP of the company several years later.

The point to this story is pretty simple. Executives' time has a value, whether we express it in dollars per year/month/day/hour or in pencils per minute. Why do you think we talk about "spending" and "saving" time?

That gets us back to the concept of the uses of time. I would love to have corporations publish exactly how their top executives spent their time in the previous year. I honestly believe that business would be revolutionized if people kept a careful log of their time and then published it annually as they do "sources and uses of funds." Virtually every executive would resolve to change some aspect of how he would "spend" his time in the coming year. Many investors would ask for their money back.

Okay, you may now ask, how should an executive spend his time?

Let me start with a general observation. The well-known 80/20 rule applies to time. We all hear about typical applications of the 80/20 rule. For example, it says that in any business, 80% of your revenue comes from 20% of your clients, or 80% of your profits come from 20% of your product line.

As it applies to time, 80% of your time is being spent against 20% of your problems/opportunities and issues/projects. The obvious question is whether or not you are spending that time working on the right issues.

Another general observation before we attempt a specific answer. In any given business, very few things really affect the business in a truly significant way. Successful executives spend their time on the Big Issues.

The next time you feel torn between Project A, Meeting B, or Trip C, ask yourself a simple question. Which one of these activities, if completed perfectly, will have the greatest effect on my business this week, this month, or this year? Follow that up with a second question. What activity, if substituted for any of the three above, would have an even greater effect over the same period of time?

Now we are ready to address the "uses of time" issue more specifically. The question is: what specific activities or kinds of activities really do affect the business? Here's my list:

- Salary Incentive Programs
- Organizational Structure Issues
- Product/Service Improvements
- Customer Trial Programs
- Customer/Supplier Relationships

•   Goal-Setting/Planning

•   Personal/Personnel Improvement

Each of these "uses of time" deserves a brief discussion.

<u>Salary Incentive Programs</u> — First, let me drop a bombshell. Many people, especially entrepreneurs, do not start a business, or work night and day, for money. Their motivation is usually tied to the desire for personal freedom or self-expression. Often they are entrepreneurs because they can't stand working for anyone else, and no one else can tolerate them as employees.

But the overwhelming majority of employees are motivated by money. That means that salary incentive programs of all kinds (bonuses, contests, commissions) are among management's most powerful tools, especially short-term.

I have a friend who is a business "fixer," a turnaround artist. He says that one of the first things he does when he takes over a new company is look at the salary incentive program. A mistake he feels managers often make is limiting incentives to salespeople. In service industries, an incentive for service providers is often the most effective marketing program available to management.

The best, recent example is in the grocery business where A&P has begun substituting a salary plus profit-sharing program for an all-salary program in several marketing areas. The results have been dramatic. In Philadelphia, where A&P had closed its stores because of poor sales and skyrocketing labor costs, they reopened under a new union contract calling for a lower base salary and a profit-sharing clause tied to lower store labor costs. Suffice it to say that service in these stores has improved, sales are way up, profits are up and clerks' salaries are up.

This is but one of countless examples where management attention to employee pay plans can work miracles. Unfortunately, most managements pay infrequent attention to this critical issue.

<u>Organizational Structure Issues</u> — Every animal must adapt to its surroundings or die. Businesses are no different. That's why organizational structure issues are so important. They are the business equivalent of Darwin's adaptability of the species.

Most businesses probably designed their original organizational structure to fit the environment in which they competed when they started. Unfortunately, many of these structures are now inappropriate because the environment has changed. That's why management needs to constantly focus on organizational structure issues.

A good metaphor for understanding organizational structure is the Indianapolis 500 auto race. On the surface, the race always seems to be the same. It's held on the same day in the same town on the same track year after year. But every year, new cars are designed. In other words, the competitive environment changes, so every competitor every year questions everything (tires, carburetor settings, aerodynamics, etc.). If an American businessman checked his organizational structure as thoroughly as Roger Penske checks his cars, maybe he would experience success as frequently as Penske does.

Two examples of organizational changes have received lots of press and serve as good examples of the importance of this issue.

For years, leading American grocery manufacturers have organized themselves around major divisions, usually reflecting a common manufacturing heritage (e.g., soup divisions, paper divisions, bakery divisions, etc.). As companies became multi-divisional, salesforces multiplied such that one company might have five different salespeople calling on the same retailer.

At one point in time, this may have made sense, but more recently, manufacturers have been questioning the wisdom of fractionalizing their power in dealing with an increasingly more powerful retail trade.

The first major company to confront this problem was Campbell Soup. They decided to change their organizational structure by combining salesforces geographically so that the retail trade saw one Campbell representative across all Campbell product lines.

Other multi-divisional companies have watched Campbell's "experiment" closely, and more recently, one of the most conservative manufacturers, Procter & Gamble, began to rearrange its salesforces along lines similar, if not identical, to Campbell. If anyone needed a clear signal of the growing power of the retailer, it was P&G's decision to change its sales structure to respond to the changing retail environment.

Oddly enough, given the deservedly conservative reputation of P&G, they furnished another recent and different example of a major structural change in their organization. A little history lesson is required to understand the importance of this change.

Since the 1920's, P&G's organization has been typified by a "division with brands" structure. As the company grew from its soap origins and added new brands in food, toiletries, paper, etc., the new brands became new divisions with multiple brands of their own. As a result, by the late 1980's, P&G had seven consumer product divisions, each with multiple brands.

Then P&G dropped its bombshell. Henceforth, the dominant organizing principle for P&G would not be the division or the brand, but rather the category. So, P&G announced a radical new organization built around categories (bar soap, toilet tissue, dentifrice, etc.) with each category having the full panoply of people, capabilities and authority to maximize P&G's share of category and profits.

P&G's public explanation for this radical shift was that it pushed decision-making lower into the organization, thereby making the company more responsive to rapid changes in the competitive environment. Other less obvious advantages were that it tended to bring P&G's management focus into congruence with that of the retailer who already thinks categories, not brands. Still another advantage from P&G's perspective was the opportunity to expose young executives to general management issues earlier in their careers, giving the company an opportunity to develop general management skills among a broader base of executive talent instead of limiting the company to general management drawn largely from the ranks of brand management.

The point of all this is that Campbell Soup and P&G responded to a change in the business environment by changing their organizational structure, in both cases making changes that were profound and probably correct.

One last thought on organizational structure. P&G and Campbell changed their structures to sharpen their focus, thereby increasing the effectiveness of existing staff. Neither used an organizational change to reduce head count, cut costs or increase profits in the short term.

But organization structural changes can often have a dramatic impact on the bottom line by combining functions and reducing head count.

My friend, "the business fixer," says that organizational restructuring to eliminate duplication and reduce head count is the second arrow in his quiver, right up there with compensation changes.

Product/Service Improvements — Nothing is more important to the long-term health of a company than improving existing products or services, with the possible exception of creating new ones. Nothing is more time-consuming than improving an existing product or service except developing a totally new one. Having said this, I never cease to be amazed at how little time most companies spend on product improvements and new products. The bigger the company, the more removed management is from this critical activity. In fact, many companies express their contempt for the entire function by putting their least experienced people in the new product area.

Successful companies, or companies that want to stay successful, need to put more organizational horsepower behind the future. Top management needs to get involved and stay involved for several reasons: to communicate the importance of growth throughout the company, to overcome organizational antagonism toward new, revenue-consuming projects, to encourage a sense of risk-taking throughout the organization.

Too often, top management plays Pontius Pilate, washing its hands of the difficult, frustrating and often failure-prone product development function. No one can estimate what percentage of his time a top executive should allocate to product development, but I can guarantee you one thing — the individuals who founded America's great industrial dynasties spent more of their time on this one function than on anything else.

Customer Trial Programs — Peter Drucker, the Austrian-born business scholar, says that the object of business is to make someone a customer. The key to making a customer is getting a potential customer to try your product or service.

Following that simple and irrefutable logic, one would think that managers would spend a significant amount of time and money generating trial of their products. Unfortunately, this is not the case. In fact, many consumer goods marketers and retailers have little knowledge of, and less respect for, the sales promotion function which bears the primary responsibility for generating product or service trial.

At HMG, we have a lot of experience in sales promotion, and I must say that it has proven to be a real roller coaster, full of ups and downs and quick, right-angle turns, with great exhilaration followed quickly by sickening downward spins (see Chapter Seven).

We entered the promotion business for three reasons. First, our existing display customers were asking for help with promotion ideas often related to the displays we were designing. Second, neither our then-existing display clients nor most other major manufacturers or retailers had significant internal expertise. Lastly, the existing, external promotion resources were pretty weak. Some were run as an afterthought by ad agencies. Others had grown out of a premium supply function. Suffice it to say, we felt we could compete in the business so we founded a promotion subsidiary.

Over the years, we developed many effective promotions, including the "Go For It, America" program for British Airways that many consider one of the great promotions of all time. Over the years, however, we, and everyone else in the business, have encountered significant resistance from client management regarding promotion services.

Specifically, some managers will demand countless speculative submissions, pay nothing for the ideas submitted and then haggle with the agency whose idea they accept.

We couldn't make any money that way, so we refused to enter speculative competitions, or we asked to be able to produce the collateral material for successful ideas at a 15% markup, approximately the commission charged by advertising agencies. We've even resigned major accounts which just weren't prepared to pay a 15% commission.

It's a shame promotion agencies "don't get no respect," because they perform a significant service for marketers. More marketing managers need to spend more time with their promotion agencies working on their promotion budget. In most companies, the promotion budget has grown much larger than the advertising budget, but I'll bet that few executives, especially in larger companies, spend time on promotion anything like the time they spend on advertising.

Customer/Supplier Relationships — Everyone has marvelled at the business success of the Japanese. I was determined to understand it, so I began reading articles about how the Japanese do business. Whenever a friend would return from a meeting with the Japanese, I would ask questions about the business transaction. How did they behave? How did they do X? Why do you suspect they did Y?

I don't claim to understand exactly why the Japanese have been so successful, but I can tell you this — they spend a whole lot more time than Americans do building relationships with their customers and their suppliers. In fact, the commercial relationships which we Americans sometimes see as almost adversarial, they see as something akin to a partnership.

As a result, Japanese businessmen spend an enormous amount of time cultivating and building relationships. I have had people tell me that some senior Japanese executives spend a preponderance of their time with suppliers and customers rather than with internal company personnel. Does any American executive do this?

I certainly can't claim that I do, but I did feel we should try to build even stronger relationships with our clients and our suppliers. We started with the L'eggs Division of Sara Lee, our oldest and largest client.

We asked ourselves two questions. What do they want from us as a supplier? How can we give it to them? The answer to the first question was pretty simple. They wanted lower prices, higher quality and faster delivery.

On the surface, these three things appeared mutually exclusive. So, answering the second question (How can we give it to them?) seemed a lot more difficult. But we thought there might be a way to square the circle if we could get L'eggs' management to help.

To make a long story short, we approached management with a novel proposition. We told them we wanted to lower prices, improve quality and tighten delivery schedules. Needless to say, we gained their careful attention. We also told them that the only way we could do so was to become more than a supplier. We had to become almost a partner.

Then we said that the key was in the way they ordered product from us, and if we could develop a more orderly production and delivery schedule, we would save money in manufacturing, and we would pass on that savings to them.

In effect, we said that if both of us can change the way we are doing business, both of us can benefit. After some study and a little bit of give and take, we struck a deal that was mutually beneficial. I am convinced we could not have constructed such an arrangement without the years of productive relationship which preceded it. But that is exactly the point. The Japanese spend a lot of time trying to create and nurture relationships which produce the kind of shared goals implied in the HMG-L'eggs Cost Improvement Program.

Recently, I had an opportunity to experience firsthand the Japanese method of cementing relationships. As so often happens, the occasion was a disagreement.

We have a Japanese partner, TOIN, who pays us a royalty for the use of one of our merchandising systems. Things had been going along fine until a disagreement arose over one aspect of their obligation under the contract. I instantly realized that this was a crucial development in our relationship, so I decided to fly to Japan to resolve the dispute.

Before leaving for Japan, I assured our partners that I would be coming alone to discuss the matter, leaving my attorney at home. The Japanese know that by using attorneys in the resolution of a dispute, you are destined to go into court where everyone loses. Consequently, they avoid attorneys like the plague. I wanted them to know that I understood (and shared) their desire to avoid the lawyers.

When I reached Tokyo, I checked into a hotel and announced that I would be staying "indefinitely." This was not true. I actually wanted to leave in a few days, but I knew that my Japanese partners would not begin serious negotiations until a few hours before I was about to leave. So, the only way to get things going was to indicate I could stay forever. It worked. The Japanese got down to hard bargaining immediately.

My study of the Japanese revealed that the less you talk, the smarter they think you are, so I adopted a difficult and very uncharacteristic tactic. I kept my mouth shut. It took a while, but I listened very intently to the seven (7) Japanese who had come to the meeting.

After sixteen (16) consecutive hours of Japanese monologue, I showed my hand. I told them that this wasn't a business deal we were discussing, it was a relationship issue. It was a question of partners discussing moral obligations which involved, above all, trust. Then I told them I trusted them to do what was right for our relationship because that transcended any individual contractual point.

The Japanese stopped talking. Two of them got up, left the room for a short period and then returned. "Mike-san, you are right. This is not a business decision. We agree with you."

Within a few minutes, we resolved our differences in a way that permitted the Japanese to demonstrate they valued the relationship as much as we did.

After we had shaken hands, the Japanese complimented me for listening to them and not trying to talk. They reiterated their feeling that we had not had a business meeting but something more like a discussion among family members, like a man and wife, with each valuing fairness and a long-term relationship more than a one-time negotiating victory that might have destroyed trust.

A few days after I returned to New York, a check arrived. Shortly thereafter, the Japanese asked if they could invest in our MarkitStar venture. We welcomed their investment and asked their president to sit on our Board of Directors.

I'm glad I took the time to develop that relationship.

Goal-Setting/Planning — One of the truly astounding things about business in America, especially large, bureaucratic business, is the amount of time spent rehashing the past. I have never understood why so much time is spent on a subject over which one has no control.

Conversely, surprisingly little time is spent by most managements in planning for the future. I am not suggesting that most managements don't have a planning process in place or don't "think" about the future. What I am suggesting is that management too often fails to participate in the process. They often approve a plan, or okay a goal, without a rigorous understanding of all the item-by-item, account-by-account, division-by-division assumptions built into the final product.

A revealing exercise for most executives would involve totalling the number of hours spent in the last two months reviewing the past versus those spent planning for the future. Surely everyone understands that two of the most important acts of an executive are setting a goal and devising a plan to reach that goal.

Most executives, even the very best, too often abdicate their personal responsibility to set goals and devise a plan in favor of late-inning criticism of goals and plans prepared by others lacking their insight and experience.

Personal/Personnel Improvement — An executive I know sets an unusual goal for himself. He vows to learn one new, major skill every year. So at the age of 45, he undertook to teach himself how to operate a computer. At 46, he took Spanish lessons, and at 47, he enrolled in a cooking school.

The psychiatrist, Abraham Maslow, spent his life studying successful, healthy, "whole" personalities. He concluded that the urge to learn and grow throughout life is a hallmark of successful people.

The same thing goes for business organizations and the people in them. A successful, healthy organization puts a premium on training and people development. This emphasis must come from top management.

A useful exercise at every level in any organization is to ask an executive, "What have you taught your people in the past six months," or "what do your people need to learn to advance?" A useful question is to ask every member of your organization, "What would you like to learn in the next six months?"

Fast-growing organizations must spend an exceptional amount of time on training, because if they don't, they won't have the skilled people to keep growing. An interesting example is Food Lion, the North Carolina-based grocery retailer. Food Lion is an extremely cost-conscious operator in every respect but one. They have a lavish training budget. At any given point in time, nearly a third of their employees are involved in some sort of formal training process.

Because of their fanatic emphasis on training, they have been able to maintain a 20+% growth rate year in and year out for over a decade.

An executive who spends time on personnel improvement will build a happier, more effective, more loyal, faster-growing company. Think of it this way. An investment in training tells an employee three things: we believe you deserve special help to improve; we believe you're important to our future; we're planning on growing with you.

These aren't bad messages to be sending employees, and that's why management needs to spend time on training.

Now that I've told you how I think you should be spending your time, do yourself a favor.

Make your own list of the activities you think are the most important in your job.

Now check your past six months' calendar against your list (or mine).

Pretty frightening, isn't it?

CHAPTER SIXTEEN
The Marketing Man & Woman of the Future

Our work style at HMG brings us into contact with young marketing executives with lots of ability and even more ambition. Invariably, these young people, half of whom are women, seek our perspectives on "what it takes to succeed in marketing."

We have been asked what can amount to the same question by top management: "How can I build the marketing department of the future?"

I used to answer my young colleagues by analyzing the specific career path open to them in the company by which they were currently employed. More recently, I have realized I was doing my young friends a disservice. They were asking a much broader question that deserved a more thoughtful and comprehensive answer. With this need in mind, I began to expand my field of vision to encompass what I now call the "marketing man or woman of the future."

Before I outline what it takes to become the marketing man or woman of the future, I have to share my assumptions regarding the future of marketing. Here are the central ones:

- Change will continue and accelerate.

- Internal corporate training will decrease.

- The line between sales and marketing will vanish.

- Retailers will grow in importance.

- Promotion will grow in importance relative to advertising.

- Computer-based expert systems will flourish.

- Internationalism will reign.

- Oral presentation will increase in importance.

If these assumptions regarding the future are correct, here is what today's young marketer must do to become "the marketing man or woman of the future:"

- Recognize that you must continuously train yourself throughout the balance of your career, and especially over the next decade.

- Design your own training program. Devote time and thought to it. Set up specific hours of your week for such a program. Keep that time sacred.

- Lean on outside vendors to train you in their specialty. If the corporation won't or can't train you, turn to your suppliers or clients.

- Every year, ask your ad agency for its list of the 20 best TV commercials or print ads. Ask the agency why the examples they have chosen are effective. Collect demonstration tapes from these agencies.

- Build your knowledge of promotion effectiveness. Understand the computer-based, analytic systems. Develop your knowledge of basic promotion concepts like the worth of a customer, transaction frequency, size and pattern.

- Collect samples of great promotions. Cultivate promotion agencies. Ask your sales department and retailers for examples of effective promotions.

- Keep your own file of articles that impress you. Subscribe to trade journals in related fields (market research, packaging, etc.). Read and clip from these sources.

- Set up a system for monitoring trends. Read one major book or article on the future every month. Subscribe to *American Demographics*. Read the proceedings of futurist groups.

- Commit yourself to learning retailing. Subscribe to the major retailing trade magazines. Develop a mutually enriching professional relationship with at least two retail counterparts.

- Understand how retailers evaluate success. Learn their compensation system and their decision-making process.

- Aggressively assist the sales department at every opportunity. Help in preparing presentations. Offer to attend presentations. Ask for task force assignments that give you sales experience.

- Understand how your sales department is evaluated and remunerated. Learn how other sales departments are organized. Look for ways to increase sales and marketing collaboration.

- Make computer literacy a fetish. Learn and utilize a major spread sheet and data base program. Learn to access at least one of the major information utilities, e.g., Dialog.

- Volunteer as marketing's representative on corporate "expert systems" programming projects. Understand the computer ordering process between manufacturer and retailer. Attend seminars and conferences on the Uniform Communication Standard.

- Choose one foreign culture to understand thoroughly. Learn its history, language and commercial mores. Subscribe to a major, non-U.S. business and news publication.

- Combine vacation and business overseas. Visit retailers and check their shelves. Have dinner with foreign-based associates of your company or your vendors.

- Build a library of business classics. Ask people you respect to recommend books. Review the reading list at major business schools. Reread each classic every two or three years.

- Build and retain a list of people you consider "special." Keep these people on your personal radar screen. Seek their advice on trends, data, issues.

- Develop a system for monitoring the personal use of time. Evaluate your use of time against certain standards. Jealously guard time for learning and training.

- Develop personal communication skills, especially oral presentation skills. Review major presentations made internally for ideas to embrace or avoid. Consider taking a class or a seminar to polish your skills.

- Develop a formula for personal written communications. Collect samples of good memos. Use them as guides.

- Find a person trained at P&G and ask him for criticism of your written work.

- Understand success. Look for successful retailers and products. Analyze the basis for their success.

- Set up a three-year plan for yourself. Focus less on what job you want or what salary you want than on the personal skills and capabilities you wish to develop by the end of the three-year period.

- Always look for the question. The answers will come soon enough.

- Learn to listen five times more than you talk.

- Never be afraid to admit ignorance.

- Prize courage above all virtues.

CHAPTER SEVENTEEN

The Future's Audit

In the late 1970's a friend asked, "How do you know you're in a business that's going to last?" I knew he had been going through some rough times, so I reassured him by mentioning all the good things his business had going for it.

"Mike," he interrupted, "I'm not talking about my business. I'm talking about yours. How do you know HMG is going to grow?"

I was surprised that he would even ask such a question. He knew we had just gotten a big order from Noxell, and that our business had never been better. Then he dropped the bomb on me. "I just got back from Europe, and they've got those new kinds of stores over there with no displays. I hear they're coming over here, and if they do, won't it hurt your business?"

I laughed at his concerns and pointed out there were 40,000 different food, drug and mass merchandising outlets in the U.S. which were using our displays, and that they weren't going to be put out of business by crazy, "foreign" ideas like hypermarkets and "box" stores. My friend was convinced by my confidence, so we spent the next half-hour talking about his business which really wasn't so hot at the time.

I forgot about this episode until one of our clients asked an almost identical question, "How do you know you're in a good business?"

"We're making the payroll," I answered.

"No, Mike, I'm serious. How do you know things are going to keep going as they have been?"

I learned long ago that when a client asks a serious question, he expects an answer. I gave him the best one I could think of.

"Relax," I laughed, "we listen to the future every day." I reminded him that we spend a lot of time in group sessions listening to consumer reaction to new products, display and promotion ideas. I pointed out that our research department spends time reading, distilling and circulating relevant articles. Despite the rising interest rates and unemployment that were at the heart of my client's concern, I assured him, "everything will be fine."

This time, however, I did not forget the conversation so quickly. In fact, it finally caused me to review exactly what the future did hold for us.

My first thought was of the "box" stores and hypermarkets of Europe. I do not consider these new formats a short-term threat to our space management display business, but they could be a long-term threat if their cost advantage forced American supermarkets to adopt them. HMG had a long-term business plan which did not include the potential negative represented by these new formats. I began thinking that if we had missed something as obvious as these new stores, might we have neglected something else?

I realized that we had a "plan," but did not have an organized "process" for anticipating and accommodating the future. What we needed was a means of listening to the future for our company just as we listened to the future for our clients.

Over the next few months, we did a lot of thinking and talking about the future with industry consultants and clients. We clipped articles about future forecasting and read books on the subject. From that effort emerged three techniques that can be used by any company, large or small, to help it respond to the future. The three techniques are:

- trend response.

- looking backward.

- disaster check.

140

Trend Response

Trend response is the most thorough of the approaches and requires the most work. It proceeds in three stages. First, you should identify all of the major trends remotely applicable to your business. Most companies would look at the following kinds of trends:

- Demographic

- Economic

- Attitudinal

- Raw material

- Technological/scientific

- Political/legislative

- Competitive

The initial objective is to identify as many trends as possible, so consult with a broad cross section of people, both inside and outside the company. This step requires time and patience to insure that nothing goes unidentified.

Next, group the trends according to their categories. This should be done quickly by a small group of people.

Then return to the larger group who first identified the trends, and have them rank the trends on several bases: their importance to the company, either positive or negative; the product or profit center most affected by the trend; the immediacy of the impact of the trend.

Expect some disagreement over the ranking. Airing such disagreements will be a revealing experience. Try to reach closure on the five trends that are most important to the company. Separately, list the trends that will immediately impact the company.

Now comes the hard part — the third step in the trend response technique. Ask the appropriate person in your organization to prepare an outline of the company's response to the high-priority trends. Believe it or not, these trend response working papers are the real "long range plan" of your company. A well-run company will maintain a process of this sort, repeating it every 12 months or so as part of the on-going planning process.

Let me show you how this process works by reviewing the results of a survey of executives in food retailing. The question: Identify and rank the trend which will have the greatest impact on your industry in the 1990's.

Rank	Factor or Trend
1.	Changing consumer lifestyle
2.	Labor and operational costs
3.	Scanning/computer technology
4.	Discount stores/price clubs
5.	Direct store distribution
6.	Nutrition consciousness
7.	Prepared foods (deli/bakery)
8.	The working woman
9.	Retail merchandising/advertising
10.	Manufacturer consolidation

When I first saw this, I was surprised by what wasn't on the list. I'd expected retailers to put improved shelf allocation and competitive consolidation on the list of Top 10 trends. This proves one of three things: (1) the retailers know their business better than I do; (2) I know the retailers' problems better than they do; or (3) different people see different trends differently.

More to the point, however, is what a retailer might do in response to a concern such as "labor and operational costs." Well, he might experiment with unmanned checkout counters as Kroger is doing in Atlanta, or he might negotiate a lower labor rate for certain jobs.

An even more interesting question is: What can manufacturers do to help the retailers with their concerns? They could offer to "partner" with retailers. As described in Chapter Six, P&G and others are partnering with Wal-Mart to drive excess costs out of one another's operating systems.

Looking Backward

Looking backward requires a knowledge of recent trends and of the competition and marketplace. This technique asks the practitioner to project himself five or ten years ahead and then look back at the marketplace as a historian, identifying key developments that have occurred over that time period. An abbreviated "looking backward" scenario for the food retailing business from the year 2000 might look something like this.

Membership warehouse clubs became major factors in food retailing throughout the U.S. in the early 1990's. They began to combine their superior software capabilities with their membership list to offer home delivery of key grocery items, as well as pickup of computer-to-computer-ordered groceries. Though not offering a product selection equal to that of supermarkets, warehouse clubs gained market share because of low prices and the time-saving convenience of home delivery and quick pickup.

Warehouse clubs continued to offer a limited selection of food items compared to supermarkets, but gradually increased selection through the 1990's. In 1994, a major suit was filed by the FTC claiming certain manufacturers were colluding with large membership warehouses, offering them prices not available to other classes of trade.

By 1995, membership warehouses stopped growing as their failure to provide fresh produce, fresh meat and smaller package sizes created a ceiling on the number and type of consumers patronizing the stores and on the markets for which they were a serious competitor.

Superstores and combo stores, with their mix of food, drug, soft goods and services, were the preferred retailing format of the late 1990's, driven by consumers' intense time consciousness that translated into more and more one-stop shopping.

Three major trends which started in the 1980's became major factors in the superstore of the 1990's.

Threatened on the one side by warehouse clubs and on the other by conventional, fast food restaurants, food retailing chains made a major commitment to upgraded deli and carryout food. Some local chains engaged in joint ventures with popular local restaurants to offer their signature dishes through the supermarket deli. Fast food franchises were enticed inside supermarkets to provide a branded presence at the deli. Major bakeries supplying the restaurant industry now brought their brand names to the supermarket bakery. The quality and variety of ready-to-eat foods grew steadily throughout the 1990's. The deli and bakery became major volume sources for manufacturers able to solve critical distribution problems.

Meanwhile, product mix and store layout continued to change. The produce department enlarged dramatically in response to consumers' desire for the nutritional value perceived in fresh produce. At the same time, the dry grocery section shrank as retailers began to reduce selection in an attempt to reduce inventory and operating costs throughout the system. Manufacturers found themselves repeatedly threatened with various fees to obtain or maintain distribution. Leading brands became overwhelmingly strong, weak brands were ignored and discarded. More old, tired brands died in the 1990's than at any time since World War II.

I could go on, but you get the idea.

The "looking backward" technique obviously involves some creativity, some guesswork, even some fantasizing, but it can prove to be very stimulating.

One of our clients uses this technique and assigns a small team to "manage" a competitor over the next decade. Then the team presents the accomplishments of its management during the preceding (actually the next) decade. You can really get to know a competitor when you're forced to "manage" its business over a protracted period of time.

Disaster Check

The last technique we use in the Future's Audit is called a "disaster check." This technique challenges a company to ask, "What is the worst thing that could reasonably happen to our business?"

Let me give you an example of how this works. Several years ago, I was listening to a speech by Alvin Toffler, the famous futurist. Someone asked Toffler about the worst thing he could imagine happening in the United States. Toffler had obviously been asked this question before (or at least he had thought about it before), because he instantly gave the following answer which I will paraphrase.

The worst thing I can imagine happening is nuclear war, but I really don't think there is a high probability that one will occur. The people who control the weaponry on both sides are rational people.

Now if you ask me the question slightly differently, for example, what's the worst thing that can happen to the U.S. which has a chance of occurring, then my answer is... a revolution in Mexico.

We are the only first world country sharing a border with a third world country — in this case, Mexico. If a revolution did occur in Mexico, millions of Mexicans would seek asylum in the U.S. We would have only two choices... turn them back, or permit millions of refugees into San Diego, Los Angeles, Phoenix, Houston and Dallas. It would be similar to what happened in Miami at the time of the Mariel boat lift... except that then, you had 50,000 or so refugees landing at one time — here, you would have five million at minimum.

Toffler's story made a big impression on me, but his technique made an even bigger impression. When I went into the office the following Monday, I began asking my partners and some of our employees, "What's the worst thing that could possibly happen to us?"

At first, I got some pretty funny answers. One partner said, "Why, Mike, the worst thing would be if you died."

My other partner said, "Wrong! The worst thing would be if you lived." (We had been having a minor disagreement over a matter long since forgotten.)

But after a while, people really got into the spirit of it, and I began to get some more intelligent answers like:

"Women could stop wearing pantyhose" (L'eggs displays were a big hunk of our business), or

"We could have another plastic shortage," or

"Chains could create policies against non-standard display fixtures," or

"Box and warehouse stores could take over the world," or

"Chains could charge installation fees on our displays."

By the time we collected all the various doomsday scenarios, we were scared half to death. No one felt all of these calamities would happen, but everyone felt that at least one would probably happen before noon tomorrow.

After we calmed down a bit, we were able to rank the calamities by order of probability and effect. Once we had done this, we were able to focus on developing insurance policies against the most likely calamities.

From the combination of the three techniques of Trend Response, Looking Backward and Disaster Check, we were able to revise our plans and make them a lot more meaningful than a series of numbers spewed out of a computer.

Perhaps more important, we had some techniques at our disposal that could help us at any time in the future when we chose to use them.

No matter how many times I emphasize to clients that the techniques and the processes are more important than the specific trends or scenarios, people always want to know what trends I think are critical for the marketers of products here in the U.S.

Obviously, numerous experts, real and imagined, have written on the subject of trends, but here are a few which seem to be the most important for the manufacturers and retailers of consumer goods in America:

- The young adults demographic segment will decrease. This means fewer entry level workers for retailers.

- The 65+, and especially the 85+, demographic segments will increase. These folks have the highest per capita disposable income in America, but everyone is fixated by their health care costs and political clout.

- The number of affluent households will increase. By the year 2000, nearly 25% of U.S. households will have an annual income of $50,000+ (1989 inflation-adjusted dollars). No society on earth has experienced such mass affluence. Most of these households will be two-wage-earner households, so they'll have more money than time.

- Health and nutritional concerns will intensify, driven by the growing number of older people and the sharp increase in the median age. The diet will get even more attention. Fresh fruits and vegetables will occupy an increasingly important part of the diet. Low-calorie fat substitutes, like P&G's Olestra, will have a larger impact on the diet than low-calorie sweeteners.

- Environmentalism, particularly as it concerns solid waste management, will be an increasingly difficult problem as communities run out of room in their sanitary landfills, and money remains hard to find for the huge investments required for alternatives, such as machinery that converts solid waste into energy. The current emphasis on recycling will continue to grow.

- Time pressure and its natural response, the consumer desire for convenience, will increase significantly. Working women will feel the pressure most intensely and react by using more services and labor-saving devices of all kinds.

- Direct response mechanisms of all kinds will grow in the 1990's. This includes everything from conventional mail order to home delivery of food to direct response via interactive television. All these activities will be driven and facilitated by an on-going, computer-related telecommunications revolution.

- Retailers will develop a much more pervasive knowledge of consumers' personal buying habits via the combination of a consumer's personal ID card (a buyer's card), electronic scanners at the point of sale and computer data bases.

- Conventional advertising, especially television, will continue to lose its clout because of the fragmentation relating to cable, the reduced efficacy of ever-shorter commercial messages and the growth of commercial-free viewing material at the expense of traditional, commercial-supported viewing. The eventual availability of interactive TV will increase viewership and viewer involvement in some vehicles.

- The retailer will rise in power and importance at the expense of the manufacturer and branded merchandise. Retailers will get closer to the customer via improved communications systems. More and more consumers will be concentrated in fewer, larger, retailing formats and organizations. Retailing management is only beginning to understand its own power. The manufacturers already know.

- As a corollary to the rise of the retailer and the decline of conventional advertising, the point of sale will grow in importance. This means more dependence upon superior retail presentation, consumer interactive devices and in-store advertising. This trend makes me very happy, because it means HMG will be in business for at least another few weeks.

I described these last three trends (the decline of advertising, the rise of the retailer and the importance of retail presentation) in more detail in earlier chapters, because they are of critical importance to all of us who manufacture, market, shop and buy. I urge you to review this information.

In the meantime, take a future's audit of your own business, using the processes discussed in this chapter. You'll be surprised what you can learn by listening to the future.

CHAPTER EIGHTEEN
The Worth of a Customer

According to Peter Drucker, the Austrian scholar mentioned in Chapter Fifteen, the purpose of business is to create a customer. That's one reason we always ask our clients, "What is a customer worth to you?"

Some clients simply give you a blank stare when you ask the question. Others will give you a qualitative answer like "plenty" or "a lot" or "they're critical to us." The clients who know their business give a much more precise answer like, "$25 in gross profit annually" or "two cases of product per year."

Some clients who really know their business can give quite detailed answers: "The average customer in the category is worth $X, but our customers are worth $X+2 because they purchase in larger quantities and their purchase cycle is shorter."

Understanding what your customer is worth to you is critical to success in business. Unless you know the answer to that, you cannot answer another basic question: "How much can I spend to attract a customer?"

Let's work through an example using a category HMG knows well — pantyhose. The numbers are made up, but you'll get the idea. Let's say that the average pantyhose customer buys two pairs at a time every three weeks. This translates to 34 pairs per year. Now, assume the manufacturer's gross profit is $.30 per pair. This means the manufacturer's annual profit from the average customer is $.30 times 34 pairs or $10.20.

Alternatively, one might find a segment of customers that buys more pantyhose per year, say 50 pairs, and that also prefers premium styles with a gross profit of $.50 per pair. These elegant ladies would be worth $25 per year to the manufacturer.

Now we're in a position to answer the second question. "How much can I spend to attract a customer?" The answer for the whole pantyhose category is "something less than $10.20 per customer;" the answer for the heavy user, premium style segment is "something less than $25 per customer."

A simple, if somewhat fanciful, example to show how this works supposes that the manufacturer could contact every pantyhose wearer in America in December with the following offer: "If you agree to buy my brand exclusively during the next 12 months, I'll give you $5 today." For every woman who accepted and lived up to the bargain, the manufacturer would realize a gross profit of $10.20, less the $5 offer, minus the cost of contacting all the pantyhose wearers. As long as the total cost of contacting all the pantyhose wearers was low enough, relative to the revenue from those who took the offer, the manufacturer would make a profit.

Every time I give this example, someone points out that no one in his right mind would make such an offer because "people will cheat and buy the other guy's brand," or "it costs too much to contact all the users." My reply is, "Congratulations, you've just discovered the trial, conversion, repeat formula."

Once you know how much a customer is potentially worth, how much you can afford to spend to attract the customer depends upon how much it costs you to generate product trial, how many users are converted to your product and how many repeat purchases you get during the year.

Sticking with our pantyhose example, suppose it costs $1.05 just to contact each user about the $5 offer, and only one in five potential users takes you up on the offer. Now each one of those who "converts" is already into you for $10.25–the $5 paid to the "converter" plus the $5.25 it cost to contact the five potential users, four of whom did not play.

Now you see the trouble you're in. Even if the converter sticks to the deal and is totally loyal to your brand, she will generate only $10.20 in gross profit. In short, you lose. Every business must understand the concept of the worth of a customer. If a business doesn't, it will eventually flounder and probably fail.

The industry that understands the concept best is the direct mail industry. To illustrate this, let me describe an impromptu experiment my wife and I conducted at home a few years ago. It all began one day in early October when I heard a noise outside the door and opened it to find my wife laden with what appeared to be magazines. She had so many that she was unable to knock on the door or ring the bell, so she was trying to attract my attention by repeatedly "hip checking" the door like a hockey player.

"Where've you been?" I asked.

"To the mailbox. It's pregnant," she smiled, proudly pointing to its progeny consisting of at least 18 different catalogs.

The next day brought still more catalogs. The week's total was nearly 50. Some pregnancy! That weekend, we began going through them. I was fascinated by the range of catalogs — one for Scottish woolens, one for car accessories, a wonderful catalog called "Everything Comfortable," full of gadgets to make life easier for older people. A remarkable variety!

Someone had concluded that we were potentially valuable customers, so we decided to figure out how they had come to that conclusion and if they were right. We identified the catalogs from which we'd made purchases in the past. We then looked at the other catalogs in an effort to understand what type of purchase would have encouraged someone to go to the expense of mailing them to us.

Over the next few years, we kept track of our purchases by mail. We watched the changing mix of catalogs we received. Old favorites kept coming, but most of those we received in the first "pregnancy" disappeared from our mailbox. New catalogs came and returned only if we used them. Others came and went unused.

The explanation is simple. Catalog makers keep near perfect records of the trial, conversion and repeat formula. They know exactly how much each customer is worth, and they know what it costs to generate a sale. If you generate more gross profit than cost, you'll stay on the mailing list. If you don't, you're gone.

What's fascinating to me is that, as a customer, your worth varies from manufacturer to manufacturer and from cataloger to cataloger. The same consumer can be worth $30 annually to a beer company, nothing to a cigarette manufacturer, $100 to a frozen entree manufacturer, $400 to L.L. Bean and nothing to a Dutch tulip cataloger.

But manufacturers aren't the only ones who can use this concept. Retailers can use it too.

For what it's worth, it appears that many soft goods retailers have been slow to adopt the "worth of a customer" concept. As recently as 1985, a leading retailer of women's sportswear found the concept completely new. They'd never realized that their best consumers were worth almost $2,000 in annual apparel purchases, but that they were getting only about 30% of their best customers' total annual purchases.

This retailer lacked an information system sophisticated enough to permit it to leverage its customer base to develop frequent buyer programs that would have generated more gross profit from its best customers. More unfortunate was the failure of management to appreciate the importance of such a system and to insist on its installation. Instead, the management of this chain, which was dominated by a fashion-oriented, "buyer's" mentality, ignored the "worth of a customer" concept and kept failing in its efforts to predict and carry the most popular styles — a risky business. Within a few years, this firm's parent company was wracked by a takeover attempt brought on, to a large extent, by the poor performance of the retail division.

Food retailers seem more sensitive to the "worth" concept, partly because their management information systems are providing them with valuable insights regarding purchasing patterns. These systems help them go beyond the "worth of a customer" to establish the "worth of a product." For example, most food retailers have discovered that featuring pantyhose is an extremely good idea. The reasons are simple. Most women wear pantyhose, so when he runs an ad for pantyhose on "Best Food Day," the retailer is appealing to every woman in his trading area.

Not only that, but women buy pantyhose frequently. Twenty-five percent will buy pantyhose someplace that week. The retailer who features pantyhose taps a large audience that's in a buying mode.

Beyond these immediate reasons for featuring pantyhose lie two others of strategic significance. The first is that food retailers don't get their fair share of hosiery purchases as a channel of distribution. Women still buy more hosiery from drugstores, mass merchandisers and department stores. Hosiery is probably the largest category regularly purchased in food stores where the bulk of the volume is still purchased elsewhere. So hosiery offers major "plus" volume to a grocery retailer. (This is true of other categories as well, e.g., cosmetics.)

Secondly, the hosiery customer tends to be a time-constrained, working woman wanting to keep her shopping trips to a minimum. She's a "one-stop shopper" who'd like to buy all she needs in one spot, provided she is convinced that price and selection are right.

Featuring pantyhose — a large, frequently purchased category — is one way for the retailer to achieve this major strategic objective. Of course, food retailers have thousands of other products from which to choose when they start preparing the weekly ad. Each product has its distinctive worth profile to the retailer. That's why every retailer must balance his ads for big volume categories, like soft drinks, bread, milk, coffee, eggs and ice cream which are bought regularly by a large percentage of households, with products like diapers and frozen entrees which are bought in large quantities by a smaller percentage of households.

As food retailers' information systems grow in sophistication, ads will be tailored mathematically by market, and even by individual store, to produce that balance of products which attracts the most customers short term and builds loyalty long term.

I have managed to get through most of this discussion without mentioning that magic word, loyalty. When Drucker said business was about creating a customer, by implication, he meant a "loyal" customer, one bound to you by the iron ties of product and/or service quality.

One forgets that brand name products grew because they assured customers of a consistent quality level unattainable from bulk goods or unbranded products. Today, in most product and service categories, consumers have deeply divided loyalties to the extent that one product can rarely count on getting a 100% share from a customer. Indeed, a product that earns $6 of the $10 worth of annual gross profit from a specific customer would be considered lucky to have such a high "loyalty" rate.

The issue of low loyalty rates is one of the most challenging now facing American business. Everyone wants a high loyalty rate, but few attain it. In many categories, no one brand commands any significant loyalty. The consumer treats the brands as mere commodities to be purchased on the basis of price or simple availability.

Why has loyalty declined? I think the answer lies in the word "divided," or rather, its opposite, "multiplied."

Consumers have not divided their loyalties as much as they have multiplied them. They've discovered that in most categories, several brands are so close in quality, there is no basis on which to discriminate other than price.

Looking at the positive side, one might conclude that this is the natural outgrowth of a highly competitive, free market system where each company's product and service is constantly compelled to attain a higher performance standard, creating a market of ten competitors with high, but virtually undistinguishable, performance standards.

Assuming this accurately describes what has happened (and I believe it does), then one concludes that our marketing system leads to low loyalty rates, commodity perceptions and lower product margins as manufacturers are forced to reduce their profit in order to buy the "loyalty" unavailable through product quality differences.

A further irony is that service businesses (i.e., retailing) have historically had difficulty differentiating themselves. Service level improvements in one organization can be matched by competitors, because service organizations lack at least one of the elemental creators of loyalty available to manufacturers — the patent. Yet in today's marketplace, retailers, especially food retailers, have actually developed loyalty rates higher than those the manufacturers have developed for their products.

Consumers do not switch supermarkets nearly as readily as they switch brands of toilet paper or canned corn. As a result, retailers are in a position to stock or not stock specific branded items with the confidence that consumers will switch to brand X rather than to store Y.

It's a dynamic, ever-changing situation, and the struggle continues, with control of the consumer and his worth hanging in the balance. The trend is clear. Retailers are steadily gaining ground while manufacturers fight to defend their historical advantage. Knowing "the worth of a customer" can help both retailer and manufacturer work together for mutual advantage. Needless to say, at HMG, we believe that in-store marketing is a critical element in the solution.

CHAPTER NINETEEN
The Perfect Client-Service Relationship

At HMG, our objective is to win all of a client's space management business and get him to utilize the related services we sell. We have a saying that captures our feelings nicely: "The hog is a noble animal."

But we know we can't start with all the business. We have to get an assignment, perform superbly and build a relationship with the client. Needless to say, a relationship is not just a series of business deals.

We give a lot of thought to building relationships, so much so that we have developed an idealized client-service relationship. From the first meeting with the client to the completion of every order, we keep our ideal in mind. We know that if we can attain anything approximating our ideal, we will get lots, perhaps all, of the business. (The hog is a noble animal.)

As you will discover when you read the profile of the perfect relationship, it mandates effort on both the client side and on the service provider side. Just as a marriage won't work if only one partner is trying, a business relationship will fail unless both parties realize their responsibilities and work to meet them.

In effect, then, we often find ourselves "training" our customers how to be the ideal client. Of course, the reverse is also true because we have learned an extraordinary amount from our clients over the years.

What are the rules of a perfect client-service relationship?

- *We're really building a cathedral.*

From the outset, client and agency must agree that they are not making bricks but building a cathedral. The client must explain how the specific job fits into the overall strategic plan of the company or brand. The agency must keep digging until it understands how the assignment fits into the overall scheme of things. Client and agency must agree in principle that both desire a long-term, holistic relationship, not one tied to a single, time-constrained transaction. The idea is to create an atmosphere of tolerance, trust and respect.

- *We'll deliver in less than 30 minutes.*

One of the main reasons for the success of Domino's Pizza is that they have a clear objective understood by everyone (the consumer, Domino's management and employees). Establishing a similarly clear, transparently understandable objective is the foundation of an enduring client-agency relationship. More relationships fail because of poor objective-setting than for any other reason. There is no substitute for a written objectives statement approved by all interested parties.

- *Two heads are better than one.*

Every relationship must have a clear leader on both sides. No agency can serve a client with two heads (sales vs. marketing, marketing vs. finance, etc.). Conversely, the client has a right to expect one voice coming out of an agency. Very early in the project, the client must confess potential internal conflicts so that the agency may try to resolve them before wasteful wheel-spinning occurs.

- *Questions mean more than answers.*

Most projects start out searching for answers. Wrong! First search for the questions. Try to isolate all the issues surrounding a project. Get some agreement as to the relative importance of the questions. In the long run, the client and agency which identify the key questions and then answer them, build the most effective, most enduring and ultimately, the most profitable relationships.

- *The truth shall make thee rich.*

Too many client-agency relationships are nothing but ego struggles with one side or the other trying to prove how (a) smart, (b) creative, or (c) powerful they are. Nothing could be less productive or more destructive. The only sound basis for a relationship is a mutual commitment to the truth. No agency should resist a test of an idea as long as it is on budget, on strategy and within the boundaries of good taste. The motto here is "eliminate personal opinion and focus on facts."

- *We can do anything.*

A good client-agency relationship assumes no constraints. The client does not tell the agency how to do its job. The agency does not sell solution A because it is profitable or cheap or "what the client wants." The agency focuses on delivering what the client needs without neglecting what the client wants. The very best solutions often come from an agency which has the courage to give the client the medicine it needs instead of the placebo it wants.

- *Someone else is on the line.*

When the client and agency are working on a project, they are never working totally alone. At least two other parties are "on the line" with them — consumers and stockholders. Both client and agency must have the freedom and the courage to step back and say, "This isn't a good business decision," or "This really isn't in the long-term interest of our consumer." I have a friend who swears he never goes into a client meeting without visualizing a little old lady in Keokuk who is the real owner of the company. He claims it gives him the courage to "do what's right" for the client and the consumer. Incidentally, this guy has a perfect record of retaining clients, so it must work.

- *Win/win beats win/lose.*

A client-agency relationship must seek win/win customers and avoid I win/you lose scenarios. Every business situation has X amount of profit (or loss) in it. No healthy relationship can be built if agency or client is determined to milk all the profit for itself, or shove all the losses onto the other guy's side of the table. Agencies need to look for ways to reduce costs, and clients need to reward superior performance with creative compensation arrangements.

- *Lions can lie down with lambs.*

The ultimate sign of a healthy client-agency relationship is when each undertakes to train the other's employees in specific areas of expertise. Think of the positive signals this sends.

"We (agency) trust you (client) not to internalize our skills and discharge us. We (agency) have nothing to hide from you (client). We (agency) want you (client) to know everything about us so that you can help us to serve you better."

"We (client) trust you (agency) with our most confidential matters, knowing you will not betray these secrets to others. We (client) want you (agency) to learn more about our business because there may be new ways you can help us. We (client) are willing to spend time and money training you (agency) because we value our relationship beyond today's short-term project."

Let me give you some examples of how these principles work in practice. Years ago, a major liquor manufacturer approached us with an unusually specific request. They wanted a miniature wooden wheelbarrow display for use in liquor stores. The wheelbarrow was to be of such and such size and decoration. It had to be 100% wood.

We had a meeting with the company to understand its objectives. Then we visited local liquor stores to understand the competition. We designed and costed out several models. They were as cute as they could be, but boy, were they expensive. The cost culprit was the wood.

Finally, one of our designers couldn't stand it any longer. "We can design a cardboard wheelbarrow for one-fifth the cost, and it won't make one bit of difference to anybody." Someone else piped up, "...except to the client."

A heated discussion ensued about utility, quality, value, reusability, truth, justice and the American Way. Finally, I asked for a vote. "What would you do if this were your business?" It was unanimous:

we loved the cardboard version.

"Okay," I said, "we'll present the cardboard cart. I agree it's better, and besides, we'll never win the bid on the wooden cart, and we might win with cardboard. Just make me up a good wooden model to go along with the cardboard one."

A few days later, we presented. "Here's a wooden model for $25, and here's one for $5," I said.

The buyer almost had a heart attack. "Mike, what the hell kind of wooden display is that for $5?"

"Just look at it," I said. "Isn't it great?" (It was real cute — we had duded it up something slick!)

Finally, the buyer couldn't resist any longer. He came across the room and touched both models. "Damn it, Mike, this thing is cardboard, not wood."

With as straight a face as I could manage, I defended myself. "Tom," I said, "cardboard is nothing but pressed wood chips. This thing is made of wood. It's more colorful, and it's a hell of a lot less expensive. You can save $100,000 by ordering these pressed wood wheelbarrows."

A long silence followed. We got the order.

Why? Because we asked the right questions. We gave the client what he needed. We learned the facts. We assumed no constraints. We had courage.

Very shortly after this episode, we were approached by a cosmetics manufacturer who wanted some counter displays. We reviewed his needs and agreed to the assignment.

Then we began doing our homework on the category, its trade channels and the competition. We quickly realized the client had asked for the wrong display. He needed floor displays, not counter displays.

We solved the problem by designing a unit that was easily convertible from counter to floor. We presented it and told the client that he really needed to order more of the kits that could convert the counter units into floor units.

"I think you're wrong," said the client, "but maybe we can find out." We instantly agreed to a "test" which consisted of presenting the two versions to major retailers. The floor unit won 4 to 1, as we knew it would. (We had already talked to some of the same people about their problems.) The client immediately became the champion of floor displays.

Here again, we sought the truth. We asked the right questions. We got the facts. We assumed no constraints. We gave the client what he needed, not what he wanted.

We realized we were building a cathedral, not just making bricks.

PART V
Entering the 21st Century

CHAPTER TWENTY
Making It Through the 1990's

Over the next few years, marketers and retailers are going to be buried under a barrage of articles about the 21st Century (including the last chapter of this book).

The only thing wrong with those articles is that most will miss a key issue — making it through the 1990's. During the present period of exceptional and rapid change, a failure to focus now on the major issues will see many old and honored companies arrive hopelessly crippled at the threshold of the 21st Century.

At HMG, one of our great advantages is that we see today's problems through the eyes of many clients. This gives us a broad perspective that helps us distinguish between those issues that will dominate the entire marketing landscape during the 1990's and those that are mere local anomalies.

Some of these issues have been discussed in other contexts elsewhere in this book. Others have been mentioned in a minor way as they related to some of the projects in which HMG has been involved. My purpose now is to provide management with a checklist of issues to confront "on Monday morning" based upon our observations of literally dozens of companies and major transformational changes sweeping the landscape.

1. Focus on information — The nature, relevance and utility of information is changing rapidly, yet few top managers are on top of these information issues.

At a time when retailers believe they have superior information (and some do), the typical top manager with most manufacturers has scant working knowledge of the broad array of data available. Even fewer companies have a comprehensive information strategy aimed at identifying, acquiring and then comprehensively utilizing specific types of data.

Along with time, information is one of the greatly undervalued assets in American industry. Unfortunately, many of today's top managers cut their teeth in an earlier era characterized by limited research tools applicable to mass markets and relatively undifferentiated, unsophisticated retailers.

The amount and kind of data available today have changed enormously, but many top managers remain locked within a time warp, unaware of the very existence of certain data, or totally insensitive to its relevance for competing in an era of fragmented categories, micro markets, diverse neighborhoods and unique retail formats.

Perhaps more importantly, many top executives fail to realize that the typical market research manager is by temperament a somewhat bookish introvert who will not pound the table demanding more money for Project X or Y. Moreover, like all human beings, market research managers have an aversion to the new or merely different because embracing the new and different requires (1) more work, or (2) an admission that previously embraced research truths are somehow tarnished.

An even more perverse (though much less frequently occurring) problem is the research director who deliberately restricts the flow of research information to top management in order to insure his own indispensability. At least one major marketing firm went to the extraordinary step of hiring outside consultants to present a research symposium because their top managers became convinced that the internal MRD manager was deliberately preventing the adoption of certain techniques in favor of an internally developed, "proprietary" technique capable of interpretation only by the existing director of market research.

I would suggest every major executive hold an "information seminar" to gain exposure to all the data his company is currently employing and all the new techniques which are available but are not in his company's arsenal.

A full-fledged information strategy should grow out of this initial information seminar. Just for the record, our experience suggests that packaged goods manufacturers have better developed information strategies than grocery retailers, but that the balance of power is shifting toward the retailer. Conversely, mass merchandisers and department stores have better information systems than most of their suppliers. Fashion-oriented manufacturers have an almost visceral revulsion to research data because it interferes with "creativity" and "artistic judgment" which are held in such high repute in fashion circles.

2. Think category — We have reached the end of the era characterized by "brand think." We have entered the era of "category think." Approaching business in category terms helps in numerous ways. First, it helps the manufacturer align his thinking with that of the retailer which is predominantly "category think." Second, it helps the manufacturer understand the full panoply of benefits available to consumers and the position his brands occupy within the range of available benefits.

A useful exercise in almost any category is the construction of a substitutability matrix revealing what products are used in place of others when the consumer is seeking the basic benefits of the category.

Example: When consumers eat a grain-based product for breakfast, what are the forms, flavors and types they ingest? Is the product a bread, a muffin or a sweet cake product? Is the product eaten warm or cold? Does it start frozen, refrigerated or packaged? Which products are most often substituted for one another? By whom? Under what circumstances?

One extreme example of category focus is P&G's move away from brand management to an organization based upon category management. When this revolutionary change in the P&G organization was announced, the company explicitly recognized the two advantages of "category think" mentioned above. In passing, the company also expressed its hope that this revised organizational approach would speed up its laborious, decision-making process.

What the company didn't mention in public was its hope that category focus would help foster a greater sense of teamwork at lower levels in the organization and expose more people from more disciplines to general management problems earlier in their careers. P&G realized that thinking "category" rather than "brand" has a transformational effect on the way companies organize themselves and compete in the marketplace.

Therefore, one of the things management must do to make it through the 1990's is to focus first on categories and some upsetting questions about existing brands, the consumer, the trade and the organization.

3. Focus on building loyalty — From time immemorial, manufacturers have repeatedly spent millions of dollars to try to create an intense loyalty between their brands and their consumers. Ideally, that loyalty is so strong that a consumer will go to another store rather than buy another brand in a store not carrying the favored product.

Few brands inspire that kind of loyalty, and few manufacturers really focus on *understanding the components and limits of brand loyalty*. Big budgets are allocated to various research techniques, but some companies will go years without doing any original thinking on how to create loyalty.

Why aren't we surprised to learn that these small companies spend millions to "bribe the retailer" to keep their product in stock? Lacking any concept of what makes consumers loyal, they are forced to purchase the affection of the retail trade. Meanwhile, the retailers are laughing up their sleeves, because it is in their interests to destroy all vestiges of brand loyalty in favor of store loyalty.

One of the key objectives management must achieve in the 1990's is to increase loyalty levels (dare we say brand loyalty?). That can't be done until top management demands that the organization focus on loyalty, know what it is, why it is and how it can be improved.

The single most underquoted fact in business is this: the brands with the highest loyalty levels also have the highest profit levels.

Why isn't this simple, indisputable truth burned into every desktop in America?

Why doesn't everyone spend every waking moment trying to increase loyalty levels?

4. <u>Co-market the categories</u> — One of the most consistent themes of this book has been the increasing power of the retailer. A related theme has been the struggle between the retailer and the manufacturer for a bigger share of the total profit pie. A manufacturer contemplating these two themes could justifiably develop a somewhat pessimistic view of the future.

The remedy for pessimism is co-marketing. Co-marketing basically means that the manufacturer adopts an objective of increasing the retailer's volume and profits of the category by helping the retailer market the category more effectively. To accomplish this simple objective, the manufacturer must be prepared to get closer to the retailer, to share information, and to align systematically with the retailer in a more intimate, multi-functional way.

The essence of co-marketing is a change in attitude on the part of retailer and manufacturer. One manifestation of this change in attitude is a change in the relationship from one of adversary to one of partnership. The result of this partnership is an increase in the size of the profit pie for both manufacturer and retailer.

Both retailer and manufacturer have powerful incentives to make the attitude changes which are at the heart of co-marketing. At the same time, both are subject to short-term, day-to-day forces which pull them back into old patterns of behavior.

In the 1990's, one of top management's jobs will be to identify and overcome those internal forces which discourage co-marketing. This means questioning everything from compensation schemes and organizational relations to promotional plans and accounting policies.

I am under no delusions that co-marketing will suddenly transform vendor-retailer relations. As one of my friends said, "Food Lion will be your partner until someone else has a lower price this month." But even the hardest-nosed, most intransigent retailer will eventually give you a fair hearing if he is convinced you know how to help his business. Moreover, if this retailer does not adopt those well-conceived programs being presented by you and others, he will eventually find himself losing consumers.

It is no coincidence that one of the world's most successful retailers, Wal-Mart, has also been among the leaders in encouraging closer vendor relations. The "partnership" between Wal-Mart and other vendors has been discussed elsewhere in this book. Few people are aware, however, of Wal-Mart's so-called Vendor Store, a fascinating experiment on co-marketing.

In these experimental stores, vendors (that's retailer talk for manufacturers) are given wide latitude in merchandising their respective departments. In effect, they are told, "Here's your space; now show us how to increase the business." Wal-Mart imposes only two significant "rules:" merchandise must be priced according to Wal-Mart policies, and whatever is tried in the experiment must be suitable for rollout to all Wal-Mart stores.

HMG is working with several clients to install new merchandising concepts in these test stores. We are monitoring what other manufacturers are trying in these stores. This much we can say already: manufacturers and consumers are very enthusiastic about the experiment.

At the heart of this experiment is Wal-Mart's belief that some manufacturers might know something about their categories that would increase Wal-Mart's volume and profit. Once other retailers realize Wal-Mart's belief is correct, co-marketing will be here to stay.

> 5. Understand profitability — When HMG was acquired by Saatchi, we periodically hosted seminars for our new owners to "explain" the business. This was a euphemism for giving the new owners enough knowledge so that they could "manage" us. In the process, these intelligent outsiders began to ask lots of questions about our business, and because they were both very intelligent and very ignorant, they asked questions in different ways.

At the heart of their questions was the issue of profitability. What drives profitability? How do you measure the components of cost? No one stays in business very long without producing a profit, but lots of people, including HMG, periodically lose touch or lose perspective on profitability. Over the years, we embrace policies or procedures which outlive their usefulness or even work counter to their original objectives.

Let me repeat one example that will drive this point home. When Wal-Mart and P&G were exploring their partnership concept, both agreed that they "probably" had adopted some policies which were driving up the costs of their total business relationship. People were assigned to explore the business relationship and the systems set up to control it.

Legend has it that P&G was shocked when they began to realize all the extraordinary cost they had built into their system to service Wal-Mart. Then they realized they simply had never previously looked at their business on an account-by-account, step-by-step, cost-by-cost basis. Everything was aggregated for the total business but without regard for costs generated at the customer level by various service components.

At some point in the proceedings, P&G realized it was handwriting hundreds of orders annually for Wal-Mart and checking Wal-Mart's credit after each order. Even Wal-Mart found this somewhat humorous, and this discovery served as a useful prod to poke for other far more costly, but equally fundamental, practices built into the system.

Sometimes a rigorous review of various practices will uncover facts that seem to defy logic. One of our clients had found that their manufacturing costs for food item A were somewhat less than for item B, even though A was nearly 60% larger and contained virtually identical ingredients and packaging. No one had compared line speeds and downtime between the two products because they were manufactured at different plants and sold by different salesforces to different classes of trade.

I am not a cost accountant. In fact, I have often been accused of not being able to count. But I do know one thing — businesses pick up costs the way ships pick up barnacles.

Every now and then, you've got to pick the business out of the water and look for barnacles. It helps if you look at the business in new ways and with new eyes. At HMG, for example, we expect that our clients will periodically put our designs out to bid with other manufacturers. I can assure you that this practice helps us keep a close eye on costs and profitability.

Unfortunately, not all our clients or other large companies go through such a direct competitive comparison with the same frequency we do. As a result, costs creep into the system, lie down and sleep for years.

6. Look for the (nearly) invisible advantages — In their darker moments, many of my clients moan about the lack of product difference which is, according to them, eroding consumer loyalty, reducing profitability and empowering the retailer at the expense of the manufacturer.

Over dinner one evening, one of my clients was beating this conversational drum when I stopped him. "Wait a minute. Your product is different and it is superior. I've seen the tests. Think how much better a manager than you your competitor has to be to survive with that product line. What would you do if you were in his shoes?"

My client immediately began to tick off a number of things his competitor could do to hurt him. Everyone at the table chimed in with a suggestion or two. As the list got longer, some of the suggestions got pretty silly. Finally, one of our dinner companions added, "These are pretty small changes."

Then my client answered, "Yes, but it's a damned long list."

I took the list, glanced down it and handed it back to my client. "These are all things you say he could do to hurt your business. How many of these things could you do to him?"

He ran his eye down the list. "Almost every one," he said. "But we've never gotten around to things like this, because we've been focusing on the larger issues. Of course, if he or we did all these things, they would amount to a large issue."

My client had just discovered one aspect of the concept of "total quality:" looking for a series of small improvements which, taken together, comprise a major breakthrough in quality, cost and customer satisfaction.

The 1990's will be the decade of total quality where companies will question their processes and systems, looking for ways to design out errors and design in customer satisfaction. I call it looking for the (nearly) invisible advantages, the little improvements which combine to give the customer a sense of satisfaction that will transform itself into loyalty.

I urge you to make a list of all the things you could do to create a competitive advantage for yourself without improving the basic product in any way. In my experience, such an exercise quickly leads you to question every aspect of the business relationship, from order and delivery schedules to warehousing practices and data sharing.

One of the basic disciplines we built into our business at HMG is a store audit. This involves the simple practice of going to a store, watching the product being taken from a case, stacked on shelves and then watching consumers pick up the product and read the label. We're looking for the little advantages, the small differences that add up to "total quality" in the minds of the retailer and consumer.

Every product-oriented company should have the equivalent of store audits in every aspect of their business. This kind of simple focus on every step in a specific segment of the business relationship chain is the best way to look for and find the (nearly) invisible advantages.

7. Redesign, reconfigure and redeploy the organization —
Business organizations are like living organisms. They adopt the configuration needed to survive. Biology teaches us that as the external environment changes, the organism must change if it is to survive.

Most businesses have an organizational structure dictated by the environment of the 1950's and 1960's. The environment of the 1990's is vastly different. Therefore, organizations must adapt or die.

By far, the two most interesting organizational changes in the 1980's within my world were those of Campbell and P&G. Although the two organizations were quite different, they did evolve along similar lines, suggesting that both independently arrived at certain common assessments about the environment.

Specifically, they became more focused on individual customers than sales geography, organizing themselves so that their customers could understand them and interact with them quicker and easier.

Secondly, they began to move decision-making authority closer to the customer and out of the mist and swamp of the home office.

Lastly, they began to transform the contact with the trade from a one-dimensional, salesmen/buyer paradigm to a much different, multi-functional contact paradigm.

I am sure both of these companies, and every other company that is similarly adjusting to the new environment, are learning something new every day. I'm also sure that no one "has it right."

I am certain, as well, that these companies are correctly reading the environment of the 1990's. It is characterized by stronger retailers, by the need for quicker responses and by the imperative to understand the retailer as a complex, living organism, not just as a buying point.

One clear demand of organizational changes is the need to reexplore job titles, job descriptions and career paths. Is a "salesman" still a salesman, or is he an "account manager?" If I am an accountant on an account team, am I in the "accounting" department or the "sales" department? God forbid, am I a closet salesman?

How is my performance evaluated? What constitutes a promotion? Should I welcome a lateral move from "accounting" to "sales" or "logistics?"

Again, one of the "hidden agendas" in P&G's recent sweeping organizational change was to expose employees from various disciplines to general management issues early in their P&G careers. This way, P&G could identify and promote non-marketing types to general management, thereby assuring a professional balance in the 21st Century top management structure, correcting a 20th Century imbalance in favor of marketing types.

Tearing apart and reconfiguring an organization is not easy. In fact, it is risky. But maintaining the status quo is more of a risk. As your competitors reconfigure their organizations, their acts of reconfiguration change the competitive environment.

I am not advocating your company's joining the "organization of the month club" or adopting some new scheme because Company A, Professor B or Author C (me) gives you permission to do so. I am

171

urging you to look closely at the organizational structure you inherited from the leaders of the 1950's and 1960's. Is this the best organization for the year 2000? Is it the best organization for today?

8. Reemphasize the human resource — American business has been spoiled by having a constantly expanding work force of relatively well-educated, highly-motivated workers.

Our luck runs out in the 1990's. The tide of highly motivated, female workers into the marketplace will crest. The number of institutionally trained, well-educated workers will not keep pace with the demand. The majority of new employees entering the work force will be those with special problems, single mothers, minorities and immigrants of all kinds.

Many businesses will find themselves competing to hire employees they would have rejected as recently as 1985. Many large businesses will find themselves in the remedial education business, teaching reading, writing and arithmetic (and algebra) to employees who are deficient in these areas but eager to learn.

Top executives will find themselves spending more and more time on human relations issues like health care, productivity, child care, etc. Visionary companies will start cycling their best executives through the human resource function so that they may understand the problems in this area and, we would hope, solve a few.

9. Focus on the point of sale — At this point, the reader is permitted to point in my direction and accuse me of shameless, self-serving propaganda. I plead guilty. But I'm also right.

Every marketing tactic normally used by mass marketers will be somewhat weaker in the 1990's than it was in the 1970's and 1980's except one: tactics at the point of sale. Perhaps sometime in the early 21st Century, highly targeted, computerized techniques, combined with television, will materially reduce the effect of the point of sale, but, in the meantime, in the 1990's, the point of sale will grow in importance.

Shoppers are more and more harried. They plan less (only 31% now use shopping lists vs. 40% in 1977). The number of purchase decisions made in the store has increased to between 60% & 80%. Every study indicates that display is the most effective and efficient marketing device for virtually every category.

At the same time, the retailer's and the manufacturer's capability to enhance the product mix by category at the individual store level is light years ahead of what it was ten years ago. Simple, easy-to-understand changes in categories can generate remarkable increases in turns, improvements in out-of-stocks and increases in return on capital employed.

While these changes in data collection and manipulation have occurred at retail, at the manufacturer and within the data processing fraternity, companies like HMG have made great strides in understanding how the shopper shops, how she (and he) processes data at the point of sale and how to reconfigure a shelf set to maximize turns, profitability and the "shoppability" of a category.

Let me give you an example to dramatize the value of focusing on the point of sale. We have a major client whose business has been under very serious attack from competition, retailers and negative consumer attitudes. They have spent millions of advertising dollars and hundreds of man-hours to stop the downward spiral of their business.

We were asked what we could do at the point of sale to help. We designed a simple device and tested it in a matched panel of 20 stores (similar stores with and without our shelving system). Our system increased total brand sales and the sales of the entire category in which our client competed. For six million dollars, they can outfit virtually every major outlet in America with an in-store merchandising system that will work 24 hours a day. More importantly, it will work at the first point many customers ever see their product (the point of sale), and it will work at the most important point for every single, prospective purchaser (the point of sale).

This is a true, but not isolated, example. Every company I know would benefit by transferring some portion of their advertising or trade-spending budget to a trade-merchandising budget. Day after day, year after year, we must prove these systems work when most marketers refuse to hold their advertising and promotion expenditures to a similar standard. In the 1990's, they will no longer have this luxury. Conventional advertising and promotion will lose so much of their effectiveness that all top executives will look for other places to spend discretionary money. During the 1990's, the point of sale is that place.

Many alternatives will offer themselves at the point of sale. Some will involve electronic interactive solutions to supplement absent or inadequate sales help in information-intense categories. Some will involve shelving systems to help the time-pressed shopper find her way through a multi-product category. Others will involve new electronic advertising technologies that don't fit conventional advertising categories.

Whatever the alternatives at the point of sale, they will deserve the same attention, respect, patience and financial commitment previously lavished upon conventional advertising and promotion.

So, that is my "short list" of required activities for making it through the 1990's in the marketing profession:

- Focus on information.

- Think category.

- Focus on building loyalty.

- Co-market the categories.

- Understand profitability.

- Look for the (nearly) invisible advantages.

- Redesign, reconfigure and redeploy the organization.

- Reemphasize the human resource.

- Focus on the point of sale.

Every HMG client (and HMG itself) is deeply involved in these activities. I hope that means we all make it through the 1990's.

CHAPTER TWENTY-ONE
The Wearin' of the Green

O̲ne of the things I learned in Europe will, I am sure, have a major impact on all of our lives here in the U.S. within the next decade.

It all started in the midst of an embarrassing confusion on my part. I was in Germany attending a trade show when, at a break in the action, I took a walk outside with one of the German exhibitors. We rounded a corner, and there in the town square was a huge crowd of agitated Germans all dressed in green — green hats, green arm bands, green shirts. For a moment, I thought I had stumbled into the Emerald City of Oz or a weird St. Patrick's Day Parade.

A speaker with a bullhorn was whipping the crowd into a frenzy, raging and foaming about something which, with my limited knowledge of German, I could not decipher.

I turned to the German vendor who was walking alongside me and asked him what was going on. "Oh, it's the Greens," he said, assuming I knew what he was talking about. Then he added, "The Environmental Party - they are a real factor here in Germany."

I remembered hearing about the so-called Green Movement, but I had only a very dim idea about their party platform or the size of their movement. The one thing I was sure of was that the people in that square really cared about what the speaker was saying. Every few sentences were punctuated with loud applause, cheers and arm-waving.

On my way back to the trade show, I picked up some literature, and

I was able to figure out that it contained a discussion on air pollution, water pollution and solid waste. I stuck it in my pocket and forgot about it.

Six months later, I was eating lunch with a friend of mine who, by coincidence, is a councilman in one of the small communities on Long Island. He looked a little unhappy, so I inquired as to his health. "Oh, I'm okay," he said, "but I've got to go to a town council meeting this evening."

"Are you always this unhappy when you go to one of your council meetings?" I asked.

"No," he replied, "but we've got a real problem that we can't solve."

"Taxes?" I asked.

"Garbage," he replied.

"Pickup?" I asked.

"Disposal," he answered. "We're out of room in our landfill, and there's no place for us to take the garbage."

I tried to make a joke by suggesting that I had a large barge he could rent.

My friend became very agitated with me. "Mike, this is no joke. Garbage is a big problem, not only for us but for everybody. It won't be very long before it'll affect your town and your business. You wait and see," he predicted.

I forgot about that conversation, too.

A few months after that, a friend of mine who's involved in politics in a southern state told me about a meeting he had attended in which all of the county chairmen from around the state were asked to name the top four issues in their counties for the decade of the 1990's. According to him, the top four issues mentioned by these county chairmen were education, jobs, drugs and waste disposal.

I was really surprised to hear waste disposal mentioned in the same breath as education, jobs and drugs which I knew were big problems.

Suddenly, the Green rally in Germany flashed through my mind and then came the discussion with my friend, the councilman from Long Island.

The next day, I read that Vermont wanted to ban the use of disposable diapers because they were unsafe for the environment. That really got my attention. Since then, I have become increasingly convinced that we have a major problem with solid waste management in the U.S. Please understand, I'm not talking about nuclear waste, but I'm also not talking about some runaway garbage barge. I am talking about the management of the disposal of packages, containers, bottles and bags that we use and discard every day of our lives.

During the remarkable political events at the end of 1989 in Eastern Europe, one of the continuing themes discussed by the ordinary citizens of Eastern Europe was the horrible destruction of the environment for which the Communist regimes were responsible. The pictures coming out of Eastern Europe showed whole forests destroyed and rivers where no self-respecting trout had been seen for years.

I believe that environmental concerns, especially solid waste management, will be one of the major problems which we, as citizens and businesses, will have to overcome in the 1990's.

At HMG, we are now doing our best to sensitize our clients to the growing consumer and political concern over solid waste management. This is an area in which I believe the public is ahead of the politicians and the business community. This is also an area where the ordinary citizen can have a significant impact by voting with his pocketbook for those manufacturers who design products and packages that are safe for the environment. Trust me when I tell you that manufacturers will respond. Some of the more enlightened ones already have.

One of these is Sara Lee Corporation, maker of the well-known Hanes and L'eggs brands of pantyhose.

There is not a woman of shopping age in this country who isn't familiar with L'eggs, the pantyhose that comes in an egg. For over twenty years, this package has been a part of American culture, vying with the original Coca-Cola bottle for the title of the most well-known packaging shape ever created. Yet, on July 9, 1991, L'eggs announced that it would abandon this landmark package forever. To quote the L'eggs news release (italics mine):

"The *plastic egg package* that helped L'eggs revolutionize the women's hosiery market will be succeeded by a design that maintains the well-known egg shape while it responds to *consumer preferences for a more contemporary, progressive package that eases hosiery shopping.* The new package features style, size and shade information that is easier to discern. It also allows for more convenient handling.

"The package will be a single-piece, paperboard carton that features L'eggs' signature dome-shaped egg in silhouette form. Modified graphics prominently display color, size and style information.

"As an added benefit, the new package will be made of *recycled paperboard* and, as with the current packaging, *all materials will be recyclable.*"

As you already know, L'eggs has been a long-standing client of HMG. A package redesign would obviously have profound ramifications on the in-store marketing plans for L'eggs, so it was not surprising for HMG to be given the assignment to "redesign the whole L'eggs package." Nevertheless, although this job was basically one that was a labor of love, it also scared the dickens out of us. Just imagine being given the assignment to redo a package that has become symbolic in the American culture and one that is part of case studies at the Harvard Business School and other universities.

HMG worked for over two years in complete secrecy designing this new package. For such an assignment, you can bet we used all the appropriate disciplines of in-store marketing as described in Chapter Ten. There was an important tradition to uphold here, even though we were obviously going to have to plow new ground.

L'eggs pantyhose is one of the best-known, early examples of a total program being greater than the sum of its parts.

In the original marketing plan, written in 1969 before the brand even had a name, the in-store marketing strategy (although it was not called that at the time) was clearly stated: "The name, package and display will work together as an entity." A package designer named Roger Ferriter, of Lubalin, Smith and Carnase in New York, took this guideline and several others and came up with the name, as well as the initial concepts for the packaging and the first display. Each of

178

the elements had obvious strengths of its own. The name was intriguing, with its unique play on words and its clever use of an apostrophe to suggest a French fashion flair. The egg package was a toy-like novelty, but also more than that, because it used one of nature's most pleasing shapes, and a subtly feminine one at that. The original "spinner" display, which was also built in the shape of an egg, "exploded" to reveal eight rotating trays of product. Even the L'eggs logo itself carries a suggestion of baby chicks and egg shapes in the two "g's" of the brand name, further reinforcing the overall idea.

During the introductory years, every L'eggs TV commercial, magazine ad and newspaper ad carried a picture of the L'eggs package and the display.

Would L'eggs have been successful if merchandised on standard supermarket gondola shelving instead of its special display? Probably. Would L'eggs have been a success in standard, flat cardboard, hosiery packaging? Probably. Given a clever package and display, would it have been successful with a boring brand name like, say, "New Sheer?" Maybe. Remember, there were other elements at work here. The product was excellent, the price was right, and nationally advertised, quality-branded pantyhose had never been consistently available in supermarkets and drugstores before.

Nevertheless, when The Howard Marlboro Group won the assignment to work with Roger Ferriter, the L'eggs marketing people and ad agency, Dancer Fitzgerald Sample (now part of Saatchi & Saatchi), to translate the original concepts into an in-store reality, the total results of all the elements working together were dynamite. In fact, excitement ran so high around the L'eggs offices that people were saying the L'eggs eggs could have contained buffalo chips instead of pantyhose, and the program still would have been a success. (Of course, in that case, no one would have counted on a lot of repeat purchases, I'm sure!)

Finally, let me assure you that all this didn't just "happen." There was extensive research conducted among consumers and the retail trade, leading to the development of the strategies and objectives from which Ferriter and Howard worked. There was additional research to test the creative ideas (package and display mock-ups, etc.) that were developed. And there was, and continues to be, research to stay up to date on how the elements actually perform in the marketplace. Over the years, new ideas have been tested, and changes have been made based upon the results or on the need for response to the changing marketing environment.

A critique of the L'eggs packaging from a manufacturing and in-store marketing standpoint would indicate the types of problems the L'eggs people tried to address over the years:

1. limited space and graphic design alternatives available on the paperboard cylinder to communicate brand, style, shade and size information.

2. because of the slope of the gravity-feed shelves of the L'eggs in-line display, the difficulty of reading graphics on lower shelves because they are facing the floor instead of up toward the consumer.

3. less than optimum space efficiency in shipping and on the displays.

4. perceived environmental impact of the plastic egg.

5. inability to automate the placement of the pantyhose into the eggs.

6. high materials cost.

(Of course, I have not listed all the positive attributes of the L'eggs packaging which, over the years, have far outweighed the drawbacks in the overall marketing equation.)

Until now, the drawbacks had been addressed on a piecemeal basis. The plastic eggs and cardboard cylinders were made of thinner and thinner materials. Construction of the cardboard cylinder and bottom disc was automated, although egg-filling and loading itself never was. The use of clear eggs instead of colored ones on some styles saved material costs and reduced manufacturing SKU's while making consumer shade selection easier. Graphic appeal and communications on the cylinders were also improved over time.

While L'eggs never received any real pressure from environmentalists, it was an issue with L'eggs management from the beginning.

Although the packaging has always been recyclable, recycling facilities were not much in evidence in the early years. Instead, focus was on the "reuse" of the egg and cylinder packaging. L'eggs commissioned the publication of two excellent books on the use of the packaging in crafts, and over the years, the eggs have been the subject of thousands of projects by women's clubs, youth organizations, civic groups and others.

L'eggs even experimented with biodegradable eggs which would decompose in sunlight. Test and control eggs were placed on the roof of the pantyhose factory where they would be exposed to the ravages of the North Carolina summer sun. Of course, countless other manufacturers were also conducting similar experiments with plastic packages and bags before the fallacy dawned on everyone, i.e., sunlight won't penetrate a landfill!

Later, unsuccessful attempts were made to make the eggs out of *papier mache*. Even though these ideas didn't work, they did demonstrate L'eggs' commitment to corporate citizenship in not sitting idly by, ignoring environmental concerns.

This brings us to the new package.

Until now, despite the issues facing the package, any movement away from the egg itself had been met with heavy resistance from senior management at L'eggs and Sara Lee. These people are the "gatekeepers" of the brand image that is so strongly represented by the egg. For many years, L'eggs has had promotional and permanent multi-packs which fit on the display. These are rectangular, paperboard packages with pictures of eggs on them, but they are not egg-shaped themselves. The company "gatekeepers" established policies limiting how many facings on the L'eggs display could be occupied by these non-egg multi-packs versus the real egg! This was an excellent example of a "non-negotiable" part of an in-store marketing vision.

So, why the change? Why the departure now? The answer is, in a word, "shoppability."

L'eggs was not bowing to pressure from the Green Movement, although a more environmentally sound package was one of the objectives and is certainly an important benefit. In fact, this project was code-named "Operation Green Pack."

Nor were L'eggs' management giving in to bottom line profit pressure during the 1990-1991 recession to come up with a money-saving package, although, again, materials cost savings and automaticity were key objectives as well.

No! I am happy to say the factor that turned the tide at L'eggs and Sara Lee headquarters in Winston-Salem and Chicago was the improved shoppability afforded by the new package design. Indeed, the HMG assignment was to lead a team of experts from HMG, L'eggs marketing and L'eggs manufacturing with one charge: how to make the shopping experience easier. Objectives addressing materials and labor costs and environmental concerns were important but not primary.

I won't go into all the techniques we used to develop this package, but here are some of the highlights. First, we did photo audits. We didn't just look at the competition. We looked at packages from all over the world — packages of all kinds, not just hosiery. Believe it or not, we found nothing we liked.

We did believe, however, that it was possible to design a simple, one-piece, paperboard package that would meet the objectives. Not everyone believed it could be done, but we proved it.

We "comped up" eight different approaches and took them to consumer focus groups. We narrowed these down, refined them and then took them into laboratory test market situations. We performed volumetric studies to understand what improvements could be made in shipping and stocking efficiency. And we did shoppability studies to measure, quantitatively, the improvements in consumer ease of product selection afforded by the new package design.

The results were astonishingly positive. Consumers preferred the new design by a 2:1 ratio over the old packaging, and they cited specific attributes they liked, including:

• shopping ease.

• overall attractiveness.

• appropriateness for L'eggs.

- portraying a high quality product.

- environmental friendliness.

Nearly two-thirds said the new design would make shopping easier, and more than 90% of consumers recognized the environmental advantages of the recycled and recyclable materials.

Our "breakthrough" was in coming up with a design that would allow us to print information on the egg-shaped dome of the new package. Presenting easily readable size, style and shade information where the consumer could find it immediately made all the difference in the world. No one had ever been able to print information economically on the plastic egg, and even if they had, the "gatekeepers" probably wouldn't have allowed it. It was primarily this improvement, along with the meeting of the other objectives, which finally made management comfortable with the image risk they were taking in walking away from the plastic egg.

I can't think of a more fitting penultimate chapter than this one on L'eggs to illustrate the succesful application of the in-store marketing disciplines discussed in this book. By following these disciplines, L'eggs has positioned itself to make it through the 1990's with an up-to-date and forward-looking, in-store marketing plan that also promises to ease the burden on the environment.

Sara Lee and a lot more manufacturers are going to be wearin' the green. And those who do it right will be earnin' a lot of it as well!

CHAPTER TWENTY-TWO

Shopping in the 21st Century

Not long ago, I was asked to speak at a marketing conference. My topic was "Shopping in the 21st Century."

When I received a copy of the program, I was flattered and surprised to see myself referred to as "the foremost expert on retail point-of-sale behavior and a leader in merchandising techniques of the 21st Century."

Boy, could I have used a line like that back when we were knocking on doors to start the business! No one thought we knew anything or needed to know anything. We were just "metal benders."

I wondered what this audience would think about their "expert" if they had seen him start a business with a cold check, hope and one order for some metal shoe racks.

What would they think of their expert if they had seen him standing ankle-deep in parrot guano trying to figure out what to do with 500 cursing parrots?

How long would they listen to someone who invented a walking shot glass by gluing it to a mechanical toy soldier?

What would they think of their expert if they had seen him design a huge, wooden display cow which sang a slogan when you milked it (pull the other udder, it utters a different slogan)?

I think the answer is that they would think he was a little crazy and maybe somewhat of a hustler. But an expert?

How does one become an expert?

Looking back over my checkered career, I think one becomes an expert in two ways: first, by focusing on learning something new about your craft every day of your life, and second, by applying that learning to projects that are successful. The combination of non-stop, continual learning and success turns anyone into an expert on X, Y or Z.

Certainly, at HMG, we have spent a lot of time learning by watching consumers shop, by listening to consumers talk about shopping and by studying countless photographs and videotapes of consumers in the act of shopping.

And we have been successful in translating that learning into ideas, fixturing and promotions which have sold literally billions of dollars worth of merchandise.

So, I guess that makes us "experts." Now what does this expert think about shopping in the 21st Century?

First, you must think about what shopping is. Shopping is an activity in which people process information to meet wants and needs.

There are several variables in the shopping equation — the source of the information, the intrusiveness of the information, the credibility and persuasiveness of the information and the location of the processor at the time of information transfer.

The history of marketing is largely the history of the changing interrelationships among these factors.

In the pre-advertising era, much of the information was transferred at the point of sale (the store or the door of the home) by a clerk or a salesman.

In the early years of advertising, much product information was transferred to the potential customer outside the store and then augmented at the store by a clerk or salesperson.

Over the past twenty years, more and more information has been presented and processed in the store by very intrusive means (a display saying, "we're for sale") and by more subtle means (a customer pausing over an ingredients label, getting basic information essential to the sale).

The balance between the various means of presenting information has changed. Salespeople are practically non-existent in most shopping transactions. We estimate that a clerk affects fewer than 1 in 100 individual purchase decisions in the U.S. today. Meanwhile, advertising has declined dramatically as an intrusive provider of credible, persuasive information. The most that a 15-second commercial can do is scream, "Hey, look at me over here." This is not information.

Given the central role that information plays in the shopping process, someone wanting to understand shopping in the 21st Century needs only to understand where and how the information will be processed.

At HMG, we believe that in the 21st Century, infinitely more information will be processed at the point of sale than has been the case in times gone by. Moreover, much more of that information will be individually customized to the needs, desires and demonstrated purchase habits of the consumer.

What does this mean? Well, just for fun, let's recall our earlier discussion of "The Future's Audit" (Chapter Seventeen), and try looking backward from sometime in the early 21st Century. Here are some of the shopping scenarios that seem likely to me.

Faxing Out for Bacon

The mechanics of shopping will change dramatically. As time pressures increase on working couples and as gasoline passes the $4-per-gallon level (in 1990 dollars), people will be making far fewer, but far lengthier, visits to the supermarket. The stores will start returning to direct home-to-store orders — not by telephone, as in the 1920's — but by fax and by computer. Orders placed electronically will then be delivered on a regular route schedule to private lock boxes. These boxes will come complete with refrigerator compartments and freezers. They'll be commonplace sights outside the doors of suburban homes and city apartments. Once loaded by the local delivery service, they automatically lock shut and can only be unlocked by a coded, plastic card when the working householder returns home.

Surge in Space Management Systems

Another by-product of cash flow management and just-in-time deliveries: an accelerated swing to SHELF and CATEGORY MANAGEMENT SYSTEMS throughout most departments in a majority of stores. As retailers come to value the display space they control as their central asset, they are relying more and more on manufacturers for expertise in various product categories. In turn, the top manufacturers are now perfecting the in-store systems which speed up inventory turns by delivering to the on-floor shopper exactly the combinations of products (competitors' as well as their own) which meet the daily needs of each individual store.

Building Private Label Profits

Contract packing will be more closely tied into the just-in-time needs of the retailers as the symbolic relationship between chains and manufacturers grows. Computers from the retail front ends will dictate when and how many lines at the manufacturer's plant will be switched to co-packing and for how many hours. Chains will continue to get absolute, bottom line, irreducible costs for their store brands; they will also have them delivered on a just-in-time schedule that ties up a minimum of costly warehouse space. One of the hottest growth areas in contract packing will be private label, shelf-stable lines.

Retailer/Manufacturer Cooperatives

Expect a stunning development in supermarket retailing as top manufacturers form cooperative alliances with dominant chains during the next century. These new marketing cooperatives will be positioned to take full advantage of the expertise of outside consultants trusted by both parties to maximize profits for all. The increased interdependency of retailers and manufacturers will heighten the role of specialty, in-store marketers like HMG. Just as Howard Marlboro's main emphasis expanded from brand management in the 1970's to shelf and category management in the 1980's, during the 1990's and beyond, new growth will derive mainly from data management and from department and total store environment management. During the last decade, we had to stay ahead of the DPP and consumer tracking curves. For the next decade, our strategic thinking is being directed toward analysis of advanced store aesthetics, shopper psychology and kinetics, improved store traffic patterns — a whole constellation of effects so complex that few chains tackle them without professional help.

As the markets in Eastern Europe, South Africa and the Pacific Rim explode, and as market economies skyrocket there, HMG clients will be faced with promising, new opportunities to develop their brands and categories even faster.

The Return of Big Brother?

Consumer information banks. The long-touted "Information Age," which began in the 1980's, will arrive in full force during the first decade of the 21st Century. With the advent of fiber-optic cables, TV will be supplied by local phone companies, and hundreds of new channels will become available. Many of these will be interactive. In 2010, every time a consumer buys in person or orders any item by phone or interactive cable TV, his/her credit card information will be funnelled instantly into electronic data banks run by TRW and one or two other mammoth, competing conglomerates. Compared with these precisely focused, 21st Century consumer dossiers, direct mail profiles of the 1980's — which were based largely on rented lists of catalog orders or magazine subscriptions — will look like clumsy blasts from a low-powered shotgun.

Predicting the Ford in Her Future

Electronic targeting. Picture the following scenario:

In May of 2024, Ms. Johnson places an order for a health-and-diet book touted on the interactive shopping channel. Two weeks later, her interactive TV screen alerts her to a new Israeli strain of melon which the diet book recommended as the miracle cure for dry skin. If she responds to this offer, she will shortly receive other logically related offers for skin care items, cut-rate visits to fashionable fat farms, "Big Gal" apparel items, etc., etc.

Depending upon her subsequent responses to a linked chain of targeted offers, Ms. Johnson's file will expand geometrically. Her likes and predispositions will be meticulously cross-referenced and will eventually form a personal buying profile which can accurately predict, within a few percentage points, how likely she is to purchase an imported dress, a box of Washington State apples or a new Ford.

This fast access to highly convertible shopping leads will drastically lower the costs of marketing. Magazine ads for high-ticket merchandise will all but disappear as manufacturers elect the direct-to-home electronic route to sell more goods more cheaply. Only low-cost, mass-appeal items (groceries, candy, HBA, etc.) will continue to run in print ads. Because network TV audiences will continue to erode throughout the 1990's, the cost-per-thousand for commercials will become prohibitively inefficient for many products. Advertisers will follow audiences over to channels exclusively devoted to special interests (sports, news, comedy, movies, cooking, etc.) where the higher CPM's are justified by higher sales.

The Maximum Mitten

Reach out and touch that jar of Jiffy. Sometime after 2010, virtual reality technology will be perfected and become as standard as stereo sound on new television sets. This will mean that the home TV shopper — by slipping on a special electronic glove — can effectively reach from his living room, *through his TV screen*, right into the shopping warehouse scene and right onto any shelf to grab any product he wants. He can, for example, turn a jar or a can around to examine the nutritional information on the back label *exactly as if he were in the store in person.*

To further mimic reality, each shopper gets his own electronic shopping cart. As he drops an item into the cart, it's automatically scanned onto his shopping tape. At any point, he can cancel an item, and it will disappear from the tape and cart. (The far more complex electronics, which can stimulate video shoppers' taste and smell nerve endings, will not arrive until much later, around 2020. In the meantime, they can order next-day taste samples sent to their lock boxes.) At the end of the video shopping trip, the consumer's order is packed, charged to a credit card and sent by the next delivery van or held for customer pick-up later.

Despite the system's considerable expense, this startling move to ersatz reality will quickly be implemented by every supermarket chain, then spread slowly into cable-access drugstores and mass merchandisers.

End of the Checkout Line?

The incredible expanding videomarket. As gas prices continue to soar and delivery services continue to grow, fewer shoppers will visit their supermarkets in person. By 2015, <u>they will be shopping mainly by store catalogs and two-way computers</u>. To meet this electronic demand, the stores will start expanding their video-shopping display facilities; the emphasis will shift from face-to-face retailing to the stores' warehousing, computer interfaces and delivery schedules.

Again, I could go on, but I'd get too excited.

Already, for example, Andersen Consulting, a division of Arthur Andersen & Company, has a mock-up of what they call "Smart Store 2000." In this concept, consumers of the 21st Century will have personal scanner wands in their homes and will order groceries simply by waving the wand over the UPC codes on empty boxes or in a catalog. The codes will be transmitted to a central warehouse where the order will be packed and then delivered.

This means that the very definition of "the store" will change. "The store" will be wherever the consumer happens to be when she makes and carries out a purchase decision. With information availability and the myriad communications techniques, it can be <u>anywhere</u>.

At HMG, we believe we are at the forefront of this new information revolution with developments like the Clarion shelf-edge computer. We also know that far more comprehensive systems are in advanced stages of testing throughout America.

We see empowered consumers capable of accessing more choices, more information to meet their desires. We see more personalized selling in an electronic home and a computerized store.

It's so far from cursing parrots, it's mind-bending.

In fact, it's so far from metal-bending, it's mind-bending.

But then, we didn't make this jump in a day. We've been learning as a company, and we've been learning as an economy, for years. Now we are ready to put in place the next generation of shopping habits and practices.

At HMG, we intend to be there banging our drum like Abraham's little drummer boy.

Part V - Chapter Twenty-two

It will be an exciting time, so you'd better get ready.
In the meantime, go out and buy something — preferably from an HMG display fixture.

L'eggs New and Original Packaging

Marks & Spencer - L'eggs Tights by St Michael

L'eggs Tower

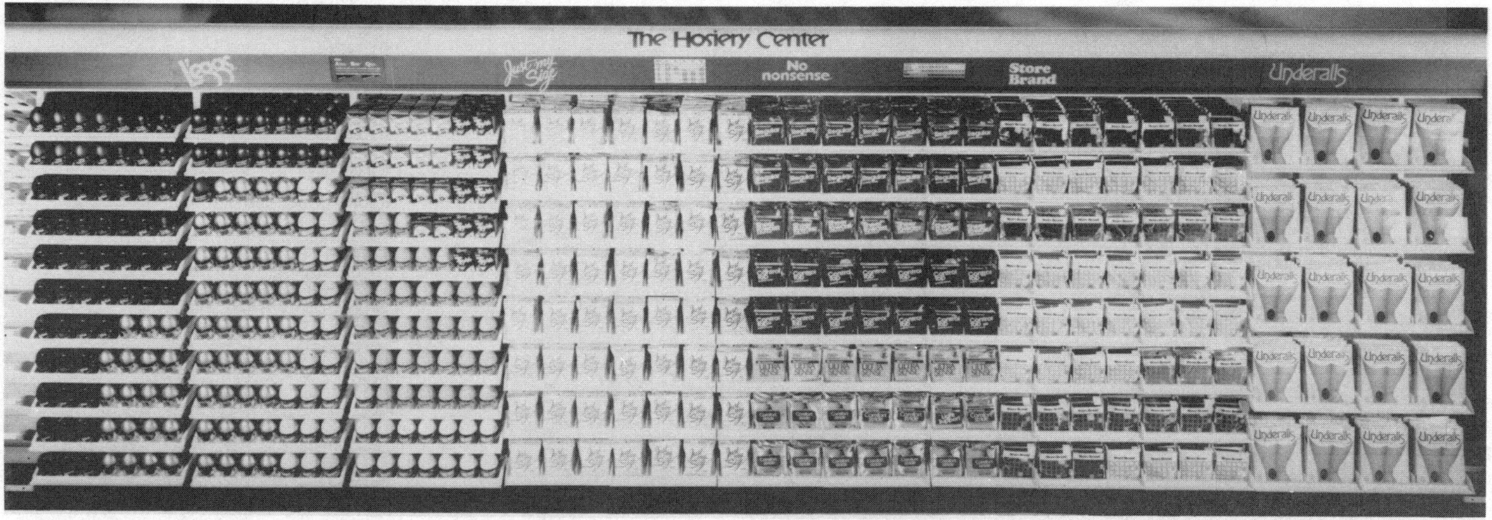

L'eggs Category Management System

Kraft Recipe Express

Pillsbury Home Bakeshop

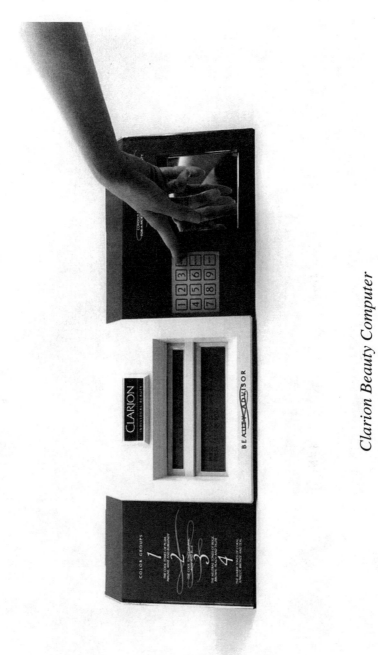

Clarion Beauty Computer

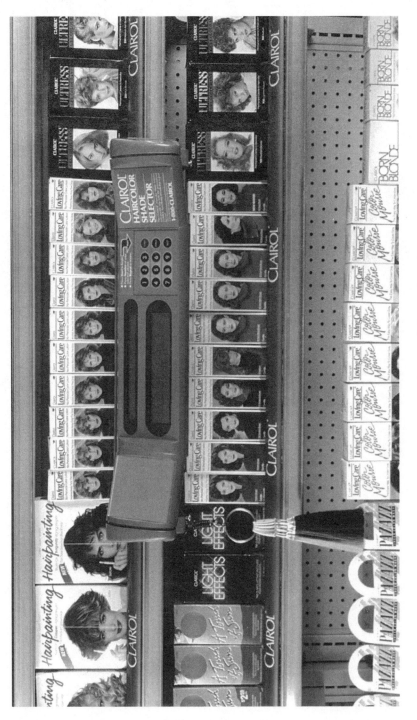

Clairol Haircolor Shade Selector

Cover Girl Uncarded Merchandising System for the U. K.

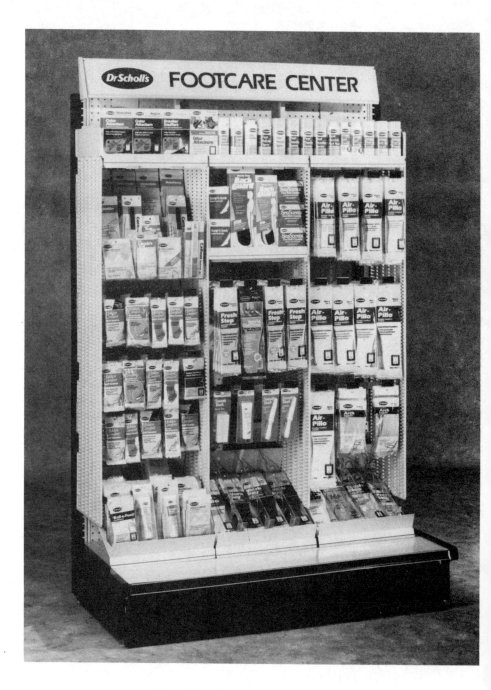

Dr. Scholl's Footcare Center